THOMAS CARLYLE'S

MORAL AND RELIGIOUS DEVELOPMENT

THOMAS CARLYLE'S

MORAL AND RELIGIOUS DEVELOPMENT

A STUDY: By EWALD FLÜGEL.

FROM THE GERMAN, BY
JESSICA GILBERT TYLER.

HASKELL HOUSE PUBLISHERS LTD.
Publishers of Scarce Scholarly Books
NEW YORK, N. Y. 10012
1971

First Published 1891

HASKELL HOUSE PUBLISHERS LTD.
Publishers of Scarce Scholarly Books
280 LAFAYETTE STREET
NEW YORK. N. Y. 10012

Library of Congress Catalog Card Number: 74-116793

Standard Book Number 8383-1035-4

Printed in the United States of America

TO

MY FATHER,

WITH

LOVE AND GRATITUDE.

" Indisputably enough, what notion each forms of the Universe is the all-regulating fact with regard to him."

LATTER-DAY PAMPHLETS, p. 253.

" Do you ask why misery abounds among us? I bid you look into the notion we have formed for ourselves of the Universe, and of our duties and destinies there. If it is a true notion, we shall strenuously reduce it to practice,—for who dare and can contradict his faith, whatever it may be, in the Eternal Fact that is around him? and thereby blessings and success will attend us in said Universe, or Eternal Fact we live amidst: of that surely there is no doubt."

EBENDA, p. 252.

CONTENTS.

TRANSLATOR'S PREFACE.

"It is well said, in every sense, that a man's religion is the chief fact with regard to him."

"By religion," Carlyle says, "I do not mean here the church creed which he professes, the articles of faith which he will sign and, in words or otherwise, assert; not this wholly, in many cases not this at all. We see men of all kinds of professed creeds attain to almost all degrees of worth or worthlessness under each or any of them. This is not what I call religion, this profession and assertion, which is often only a profession and assertion from the outworks of the man, from the mere argumentative region of him, if even so deep as that. But the thing a man does practically believe (and this is often enough *without* asserting it even to himself, much less to others); the thing a man does practically lay to heart, and know for certain, concerning his vital relations to this mysterious Universe, and his duty and destiny there, that is in all cases the primary thing for him, and creatively determines all the rest. That is his *religion;* or, it may be, his mere scepticism and *no-religion:* the manner it is in which he feels himself to be spiritually related to the unseen world or no-world; and I say, if you tell me what that is, you tell me to a very great extent what the man is, what the kind of things he will do is. Of a man or a nation we inquire, therefore, first of all, What religion they had? Was it heathenism,—plurality of gods, mere sensuous representation of this Mystery of Life, and for chief recognised element therein Physical Force? Was it Christianism; faith in an Invisible, not as real only, but as the only reality; Time, through every meanest moment of it, resting on Eternity; Pagan empire of Force displaced by a nobler supremacy, that of Holiness? Was it Scepticism, uncertainty and inquiry whether there was an unseen world, any mystery of life except a mad one;—doubt as to all this, or perhaps unbelief and flat denial? Answering of this question is giving us the soul of the history of the man or nation. The thoughts they had were the parents of the actions they did; their feelings were parents of their thoughts : it was the unseen and spiritual in them that determined the outward and actual ;—their religion, as I say, was the great fact about them."

These few words of Carlyle's, taken from his lecture on "Heroes and Hero-Worship," crowd into a nutshell the substance of his belief. It was

a belief of actions, not of words. He cared little
or nothing for what a man professed, unless what
he said was corroborated by what he did. The
performing of one's duty was the chief, the vital
thing in this life. "Too much thinking and not
enough doing" was a favourite saying of his.

In a letter to Dr. Flügel from Mr. Froude,
he says: "Your admirable little book is the first
sign I have seen of an independent and clear
insight into Carlyle's life, work and character,
as it will one day be universally recognised by
all mankind. Leaving out Goethe, Carlyle was
indisputably the greatest man (if you measure
greatness by the permanent effect he has and will
produce on the mind of mankind) who has appeared in Europe for centuries. You have seen
into this and know to appreciate it. His character was as remarkable as his intellect. There has
been no man at all, not Goethe himself, who in
thought and action was so consistently true to his
noblest instincts."

A word is needed with reference to the translation of this book, and certain alterations and
omissions which have been made.

It was thought best to omit Part I, the Appen-
dix, and most of the Notes, which deal almost
exclusively with facts in Carlyle's life so familiar
from an American point of view, and, moreover

so thoroughly well treated by Froude, Norton, Richard Garnett and others, that it would be like offering coals to Newcastle to offer them to an American reading public.

The translation has also been carefully examined by the Author, thus removing, in a measure, much responsibility in regard to it; but the final decision as to a choice of English expressions, rested with the translator, who has to thank, as well as the Author, Mr. Albert Miller, of Detroit, Michigan, for kind assistance.

J. G. T.

Ithaca, N. Y.,
Jan. 26th, 1891.

AUTHOR'S PREFACE.

"From the 'silence of the eternities,' of which he so often spoke, there still sound, and will long sound, the tones of that marvellous voice."—Dean Stanley's sermon on the occasion of the Death of Mr. Carlyle.

"Suffer me, then, to say a few words on the good seed which he has sown in our hearts" were the words of Dean Stanley in his impressive funeral sermon on Carlyle, which was delivered on the 6th of February, 1881, in Westminster Abbey—and these words express the feeling which has actuated the undertaking of the present work.

In England, Carlyle's views of life have often been made the subject of inquiry, but they have either been scattered in periodical publications, or have been partially colored, or could hold no claim of having been scientifically treated, which means nothing more, in biography, at least, than a clear and conscientious arrangement of matter. In Germany, Carlyle's views of life have generally been little considered. We willingly praised him, and praise him now, as the friend of our nation, the admirer of our distinguished men, but with that the whole matter ended, with but few exceptions.

Since the appearance of Froude's great biography, and since the Carlyle archives have revealed their treasures, it has become our duty to gather together in part the results of these investigations; and to accomplish this in the department in which Carlyle's principal work is of importance for his people and literature in general was the serious endeavor of the Author.

He has first to express his thanks to Mr. Froude, who, through his great Life of Carlyle, was the incentive to the present work, also to the estimable friend of Carlyle, Professor David Masson, and lastly, and above all, for her willingness to render assistance and information, to the niece of Carlyle, who, in truest solicitude, made the last years of the great man's life easier and more beautiful.

Before concluding these remarks, the name of Richard Garnett, which is familiar to all who have worked in the British Museum, calls to mind a small work on Carlyle, which gives in its concluding chapter a short but excellent picture of Carlyle's views. I should like to recommend the reading of this chapter, as well as of the whole work, where the bibliography of Carlyle has been arranged in its best form.

Herrenhaus, Raschwitz, near Leipzig,
  November, 1887.

AUTHOR'S INTRODUCTION.

Near the Scotch country town, Ayr, about an hour from the sea shore, stands a poor little hut, which one hundred and fifty years ago received its light through a single window that was not much larger than a quarter of a sheet of paper, when "Genius" made an entrance into it, and Robert Burns was born. What the interior of the peasant's hut could not offer, the blossoming son of the poet found in the charming surroundings of the paternal home.

One can indeed feel, when one stands upon the Auld Brig o' Doon and looks back to the old times, how the boy's dreamy and poetical nature was inspired; and if one approaches the ivy-covered ruins of Alloway Kirk and the old cemetery, the wanderer is filled with awe, as was once the good Tam o' Shanter.

Much more rugged are the surroundings of another Scotch hamlet, situated several miles southward. A single country road guides the traveller—and hundreds make pilgrimages yearly to this little village—to a very poor-looking house,

into which, five years before the expiration of the
eighteenth century, another "Genius" made entrance, and Thomas Carlyle was born.

One is involuntarily compelled to compare the
straightened circumstances in which both men
were born, and from which one of them was never
permitted for long to raise himself, but from which
the other became brilliantly transformed through
unheard-of strength of will and unceasing industry—through a strength of will which the other,
unfortunately, lacked.

The career of both men was a tragedy. If we
approach in spirit the death-bed of Burns in the
forlorn house at Dumfries, and reflect upon what
more this genius might have done for the world
and himself; what he, indeed, owed the world
and himself; what divine power in him still wait-
ed for full maturity,—or, if we enter the death-
chamber in Cheyne Row, where the heart of a
hero burst with a sigh—a hero who, to be sure,
accomplished everything which in a long and
checkered life he had been able to accomplish
before God and man; we stand by the bier of a
man who, with the greatest warmth of heart, with
the greatest strength of intellect, although his life
was spent in the most assiduous labor, was never
long happy.

But, as with Burns, in the termination of Carlyle's powerful life, there is no discord. Earnest regrets fill the heart, but they bring their own reconciliation, as true tragedy always does. I hope to be able in what follows to point out the sublimity of Carlyle's spiritual life—a sublimity from which, as from a lofty mountain, the eye discerns far and near numberless beautiful valleys—a sublimity from which the soul itself feels freer and larger.

Goethe recognized clearly the characteristic of Carlyle's aspirations when he uttered on July 25th, 1827, the following words : " It is especially admirable in Carlyle, that in his criticism of our German writers he recognises the spiritual and moral kernel as the most efficacious. He is, indeed, a moral force of great significance. There is a great future awaiting him, and it is not at all possible to predict what he will be able to accomplish."

And to consider Carlyle as a " moral force " is the object of this book. Before we turn our attention, however, to an explanation of his moral and religious views, it seems to me appropriate to consider for a moment the history of his inner life, especially with reference to its moral and religious side.

The inner life of Carlyle divides itself into three great epochs : first, his youth, which embraced the years spent in the paternal home and in Edinburgh (to the year 1816); second, those years which might properly be called his apprenticeship, when he began to fight the battles with his own nature in Kirkcaldy, the chief fruit of which is his acquaintance with the German classics; and third, the long and important period of his life which begins about the time of his departure to London in 1834, and ends with his death there in 1881.

From 1834 to 1881 are the richest years of his life, and show to the world how Goethe's prophetic word was to be fulfilled.

THOMAS CARLYLE'S MORAL AND RELIGIOUS DEVELOPMENT.

CHAPTER I.

CARLYLE'S BELIEF.

In "Sartor Resartus," Professor Teufelsdröckh, of Weissnichtwo, imparts the following ideas:

"With men of a speculative turn there come seasons—meditative, sweet, yet awful hours—when, in wonder and fear, you ask yourself that unanswerable question: Who am I; the thing that can say, I?

"The world, with its loud trafficing, retires into the distance, and through the paper-hangings and stone walls, and thick-plied tissue of Commerce and Polity, and all the living and lifeless integuments (of Society and a Body) wherewith your existence sits surrounded,—the sight reaches forth into the void Deep, and you are alone with the Universe, and silently commune with it, as one mysterious Presence with another.

"Who am I? What is this Me? A voice, a motion, an appearance,—some embodied, visualised Idea in the Eternal Mind? *Cogito, ergo sum.* Alas, poor Cogitator, this takes us but a little way. Sure enough, I am; and lately was not; but Whence? How? Where to? The answer lies around, written in all colors and motions, uttered in all tones of jubilee and wail, in thousand-figured, thousand-voiced harmonious Nature: but where is the cunning eye and ear to whom that God-written Apocalypse will yield articulate meaning? We sit as in a boundless phantasmagoria and dream-grotto; boundless, for the painted star, the remotest century, lies not even nearer the verge thereof: sounds and many-coloured visions flit around our sense; but Him, the Unslumbering, whose work both dream and dreamer are, we see not; except in half-waking moments, suspect not.

"Creation, says one, lies before us, like a glorious rainbow; but the sun that made it, lies behind us, hidden from us. Then in that strange dream; how we clutch at shadows as if they were substance; and sleep deepest while fancying ourselves most awake!

"Which of your philosophical systems is other than a dream-theorem—a net quotient, confidently given out, where divisor and dividend are both unknown?" *

"To the eye of vulgar logic, what is man? An omnivorous biped that wears breeches. To the eye of pure reason, what is he? A soul, a spirit, a divine apparition. Round his mysterious Me there lies, under all those wool-rags, a Garment of Flesh (or of Senses) contextured in the Loom of Heaven; whereby he is revealed to his like, and dwells with them in Union and Division; and sees and fashions for himself a Universe, with azure Starry Spaces, and long Thousands of Years. Deep-hidden is he under that Strange Garment; amid Sounds and Colours and Forms, as it were, swathed-in, and inextricably over-shrouded: yet it is sky-woven and worthy of a God. Stands he not thereby in the centre of Immensities, in the conflux of Eternities?

"He feels; the power has been given him to know, to believe; nay, does not the spirit of love, free in its primeval brightness, even here, though but for garments, look through? Well said Saint Chrysostom, with his lips of gold: 'the true Shekinah is man.' Where else is the God's Presence

---

* Sartor Resartus, p. 35.

manifested not to our eyes only, but to our
hearts, as in our fellow-man?"*

"For the rest," continues Carlyle, "as is natural
to a man of this kind, Professor Teufelsdröckh
deals much in the feeling of wonder; insists on
the necessity of high worth of universal Wonder; which he holds to be the only reasonable
temper for the denizen of so singular a Planet
as ours." †

" Wonder," says he, " is the basis of Worship :
the reign of Wonder is perennial, indestructible
in Man ; only at certain stages (as the present)
it is, for some short season, a reign *in partibus
infidelium.* That progress of science, which is
to destroy Wonder, and in its stead substitute
Mensuration and Numeration finds small favour
with Teufelsdröckh, much as he otherwise vener-
ates these two latter processes.

"Shall your Science," exclaims he, "proceed
in the small chink-lighted, or even oil-lighted,
underground workshop of Logic alone, and man's
mind become an Arithmetical Mill, whereof Memory is the Hopper, and mere Tables of Lines and
Tangents, Codifications, and Treatises of what you
call Political Economy, are the Meal? And what
is that Science, which the scientific head alone,

---

* Sartor Resartus, p. 44.
† Op. cit., p. 45.

were it screwed off, and (like the Doctor's in the
Arabian Tale) set in a basin to keep it alive, could
prosecute without shadow of a heart,—but one
other of the mechanical and menial handicrafts,
for which the Scientific Head (having a Soul in
it) is too noble an organ?

"I mean that Thought without Reverence is
barren, perhaps poisonous; at best, dies like
cookery, with the day that called it forth; does
not live, like sowing, in successive tilths and
wider-spreading harvests, bringing food and plen-
teous increase to all Time. In such wise does
Teufelsdröckh deal hits, harder or softer, according to ability; yet ever, as we would fain per-
suade ourselves, with charitable intent. Above
all, that class of Logic-choppers, and treble-pipe
Scoffers, and professed Enemies to Wonder, who,
in these days, so numerously patrol as night
constables about the Mechanic's Institute of
Science, and cackle, like Old-Roman geese and
goslings round their Capitol, on any alarm, or
on none; nay, who often, as illuminated Sceptics,
walk abroad into peaceable society, in full day-
light, with rattle and lantern, and insist on guiding you and guarding you therewith, though the
Sun is shining, and the street populous with
mere justice-loving men: that whole class is in-

expressibly wearisome to him. Hear with what uncommon animation he perorates :

" ' The man who cannot wonder, who does not habitually wonder (and worship), were he President of innumerable Royal Societies, and carried the whole *Méchanique Céleste* and *Hegel's Philosophy*, and the epitome of all Laboratories and Observatories, with their results, in his single head,—is but a Pair of Spectacles behind which there is no Eye. Let those who have Eyes look through him, then he may be useful. Thou wilt have no Mystery or Mysticism ; wilt walk through thy world by the sunshine of what thou callest Truth, or even by the hand lamp of what I call Attorney-Logic; and 'explain' all, 'account' for all, or believe nothing of it ? Nay, thou wilt attempt laughter; whoso recognises the un-fathomable, all-pervading domain of Mystery, which is everywhere under our feet and among our hands ; to whom the Universe is an Oracle and Temple, as well as a Kitchen and Cattle-stall,—he shall be a delirious Mystic; to him thou, with sniffing charity, wilt protrusively proffer thy hand-lamp, and shriek, as one injured, when he kicks his foot through it ? *Armer Teufel!* Doth not thy cow calve ? Doth not thy bull gender ? Thou thyself, wert thou not born ; wilt thou not die ? 'Explain' me all this, or

do one of two things: Retire into private places
with thy foolish cackle; or, what were better,
give it up and weep, not that the reign of
wonder is done, and God's world all disembel-
lished and prosaic, but that thou hitherto art a
Dilettante and sand-blind Pedant.'"*

Carlyle characterizes Teufelsdröckh's doctrines
as "Natural Supernaturalism" which might be
said to lie at the foundation of his own views
of life, which, however, we prefer to denominate
"Religious Idealism," for it is an idealism in
which a theological and religious principle plays
a very important part.

We must cite a few more passages from this
chapter on "Natural Supernaturalism" in order
to give, as far as is possible in his own words,
an accurate idea of the essence of his belief.

Teufelsdröckh deals severely with these philosophical world expounders, and discourses at
length on the physical and incomprehensible
"laws" of the universe, attempting to explain
what those same unalterable laws—"forming the
complete statute-book of nature may possibly be."

"They stand written in our works of science,
say you; in the accumulated record of man's
experience! Was man with his experience present at the creation, then, to see how it all

* Sartor Resartus, p. 47.

went on?   Have any deepest scientific individuals
yet dived down to the foundations of the universe, and gauged everything there?   Did the
Maker take them into His counsel; that they
read His ground-plan of the incomprehensible
All; and can say, This stands marked therein,
and no more than this?   Alas, not in anywise!
These scientific individuals have been nowhere
but where we also are; have seen some hand-
breadths deeper than we see into the Deep that
is infinite, without bottom as without shore.

"Laplace's Book on the Stars, wherein he ex-
hibits that certain Planets, with their Satellites,
gyrate round our Sun, at a rate and in a course,
by greatest good fortune, he and the like of him
have succeeded in detecting,—is to me as precious
as to another.   But is this what thou namest
'Mechanism of the Heavens,' and 'Systems of
the World;' this, wherein Sirius and the Pleiades,
and all Herschel's fifteen thousand Suns per min-
ute, being left out, some paltry handfuls of Moons,
and inert Balls, had been—looked at, nick-named,
and marked in the Zodiacal Way-bill; so that we
can now prate of their Whereabout; their How,
their Why, their What being hid from us, as in
the signless Inane?

"System of Nature!   To the wisest man, wide
as is his vision, Nature remains of quite *infinite*

depth, of quite infinite expansion; and all experience thereof limits itself to some few computed centuries and measured square miles.
. . . . We speak of the Volume of Nature:
and truly a Volume it is,—whose author and
writer is God. To read it! Dost thou, does
man, so much as well know the Alphabet thereof?
With its Words, Sentences, and grand descriptive
Pages, poetical and philosophical, spread out
through Solar Systems, and Thousands of Years,
we shall not try thee. It is a Volume written
in celestial hieroglyphs, in the true Sacred writing; of which even Prophets are happy that they
can read here a line and there a line. As for
your Institutes, and Academies of Science, they
strive bravely; and, from amid the thick-crowded,
inextricably intertwisted hieroglyphic writing,
pick out by dextrous combination, some Letters
in the vulgar Character, and therefrom put together this and the other economic Recipe, of
high avail in Practice. That Nature is more than
some boundless Volume of such Recipes, or huge,
well-nigh inexhaustible Domestic Cookery Book,
of which the whole secret will in this manner
one day evolve itself, the fewest dream." *
Teufelsdröckh-Carlyle then speaks of those " il-
lusory appearances, the two grand fundamental

* Sartor Resartus, pp. 177-180.

world-enveloping Appearances, Space and Time. These, as spun and woven for us from Birth itself, to clothe our celestial Me for dwelling here, and yet to blind it,—lie all-embracing, as the universal canvas, or warp and woof, whereby all minor Illusions, in this Phantasm Existence, weave and paint themselves. In vain, while here on earth, shall you endeavor to strip them off; you can, at best, but rend them asunder for moments, and look through." *

" Is the Past annihilated, then, or only past; is the Future non-extant, or only future? Those mystic faculties of thine, Memory and Hope, already answer: already through those mystic avenues, thou, the Earth-blinded, summonest both Past and Future, and communest with them, though as yet darkly, and with mute beckonings. The curtains of Yesterday drop down, the curtains of To-morrow roll up; but Yesterday and To-morrow both *are*. Pierce through the Time-element, glance into the Eternal. Believe what thou findest written in the sanctuaries of Man's Soul, even as all Thinkers, in all ages, have devoutly read it there: that Time and Space are not God, but creations of God; that with God, as it is a universal Here, so is it an everlasting Now.

---

* Sartor Resartus, pp. 177–180.

"And seest thou therein any glimpse of *Immoriality*? O Heaven! Is the white tomb of our loved one, who died from our arms, and had to be left behind us there, which rises in the distance, like a pale, mournfully-receeding Milestone, to tell how many toilsome uncheered miles we have journeyed on alone,—but a pale spectral Illusion! Is the lost Friend still mysteriously Here, even as we are Here mysteriously, with God!—know of a truth that only the Time-shadows have perished, or are perishable; that the real Being of whatever was, and whatever is, and whatever will be, *is* even now and forever. This, should it unhappily seem new, thou mayest ponder at thy leisure; for the next twenty years, or the next twenty centuries: believe it thou must; understand it thou canst not. . . . . Sweep away the Illusion of Time. . . . . O, could I (with the Time-annihilating Hat) transport thee direct from the Beginnings to the Endings, how were thy eyesight unsealed, and thy heart set flaming in the Light-sea of celestial wonder! Then sawest thou that this fair Universe, were it in the meanest province thereof, is in very deed the Star-domed City of God; that through every star, through every grass-blade, and most through every Living Soul, the glory of a present God still beams. But Nature, which is the Time-vesture of God, and reveals Him to the wise, hides Him from the foolish." *

Carlyle then strolls into the spirit-world and returns with the witty and profound discovery that in order to see a "real ghost," Dr. Johnson did not need to go to the trouble of searching spirit-haunted Cock Lane, to clamber upon church vaults and tap at midnight upon coffins—all without result, of course. "Did he never, with the mind's eye, as well as with the body's, look around him into that full tide of human life he so loved; did he never so much as look into himself? The good Doctor was a Ghost, as actual and authentic as heart could wish; well nigh a million Ghosts were travelling the streets by his side. Once more I say, sweep away the illusion of Time; compress the threescore years into three minutes; what else was he, what else are we? Are we not Spirits, that are shaped into a body, into an Appearance; and that fade away again into air and Invisibility? This is no metaphor, it is a simple scientific *fact:* we start out of Nothingness, take figure, and are Apparitions; round us, as around the veriest spectre, is Eternity; and to Eternity minutes are as years and æons." †

---

*Sartor Resartus, p. 183.
† Loc. cit.

"O Heaven, it is mysterious, it is awful to consider that we not only carry each a future Ghost within him; but are in very deed, Ghosts! These limbs, whence had we them; this stormy Force; this life-blood with its burning Passion? They are dust and shadow; a Shadow-system gathered round our Me; wherein, through some moments or years, the Divine Essence is to be revealed in the Flesh." *

"Thus, like a God-created, fire-breathing, Spirit-host, we emerge from the Inane; haste storm-fully across the astonished Earth; then plunge again into the Inane. Earth's mountains are lev-elled, and her seas filled up, in our passage: can the Earth, which is but dead and a vision, resist Spirits which have reality and are alive? On the hardest adamant some foot-print of us is stamped-in; the last Rear of the host will read traces of the earliest Van. But whence? O Heaven, whither? Sense knows not; Faith knows not; only that it is through Mystery to Mystery, from God and to God.

> "'We are such stuff
> As dreams are made of, and our little Life
> Is rounded with a sleep!'" †

"Man begins in darkness, ends in darkness; mystery is everywhere around us and in us, under

---

* Sartor Resartus, p. 184.
† Op. cit. pp. 184–185.

our feet, among our hands. Nevertheless, so much has become evident to every one, that this wondrous Mankind is advancing somewhither; that at least all human things are, have been, and forever will be, in Movement and Change." *

" Sad, truly, were our condition did we know but this: that Change is universal and inevitable. Launched into a dark shoreless sea of Pyrrhonism, what would remain for us but to sail aimless, hopeless; or make madly merry, while the devouring Death had not yet ingulfed us? As, indeed, we have seen many, and yet see many do. Nevertheless, so stands it not.

" The venerator of the Past (and to what pure heart is the Past, in that 'moonlight of memory,' other than sad and holy?) sorrows not over its departure, as one utterly bereaved. The true Past departs not, nothing that was worthy in the Past departs; no Truth or Goodness realised by man ever dies, or can die; but is all still here, and, recognised or not; lives and works through endless changes. If all things, to speak in the German dialect, are discerned by us, and exist for us, in an element of Time, and therefore of Mortality and Mutability; yet Time itself reposes on Eternity: the truly Great and Transcendental

---

* Essay on Characteristics, p, 33.

has its basis and substance in Eternity; stands revealed to us as Eternity in a vesture of Time." *

" Unhappy he who felt not, at all conjunctures, incradicably in his heart the knowledge that a God made this Universe, and a Demon not! And shall Evil always prosper, then? Out of all Evil comes Good; and no Good that is possible but shall one day be real. Deep and sad as is our feeling that we stand yet in the bodeful Night; equally deep, indestructible is our assurance that the Morning also will not fail. Nay, already, as we look round, streaks of a day-spring are in the east; it is dawning; when the time shall be fulfilled, it will be day. The progress of men toward higher and nobler developments of whatever is highest and noblest in him, lies not only prophecied to Faith, but now written to the eye of Observation, so that he who runs may read." †

" For the rest, let that vain struggle to read the mystery of the Infinite cease to harass us. It is a mystery which, through all ages, we shall only read here a line of, there another line of. Do we not already know that the name of the Infinite is Lord, is God? Here on Earth we are as Soldiers, fighting in a foreign land; that understand not the plan of the campaign, and have no need to

* Essay on Characteristics, pp. 33–34.
† Op. cit., p. 32.

understand it; seeing well what is at our hand to be done. Let us do it like Soldiers; with submission, with courage, with a heroic joy. 'Whatsoever thy hand findeth to do, do it with all thy might.' Behind us, behind each one of us, lie Six Thousand Years of human effort, human conquest: before us in the boundless Time, with its, as yet, uncreated and unconquered Continents and Eldorados, which we, even we, have to conquer, to create; and from the bosom of Eternity there shine for us celestial guiding stars.

> 'My inheritance, how wide and fair!
> Time is my fair seed-field, of Time I'm heir.'" *

These thoughts and many more which might be found in Carlyle's writings, contain the kernel of his religious belief.

The Universe, as we see it everywhere, is an infinite and divine mystery—an infinite and divine mystery are we ourselves, as we perceive the world and its phenomena confronting us. The only thing which we—a revelation of God—are able to perceive of the other revelation of God, the universe, is reverence, and worship of the Divine Being. This "Worship" before the Highest—as it has manifested itself in our souls and everywhere in the world is religion; religion,

---

* Essay on Characteristics, p. 38.

which not alone fills our souls as a sentiment, but shows itself as well in our life and works, and is inseparably bound with the highest moral beauty which is to have a sequel hereafter. That is the foundation of Carlyle's views, his belief, with which the man and all his works are permeated. From this belief spring all his thoughts and judgments; upon this foundation rests his view of the world, and all questions, solved or unsolved, which are daily agitating men's minds who crave an honest and intelligent answer, and without which, in one way or another, they may be brought to great discontent

CHAPTER II.

THE MECHANICAL AGE.

MOTTO: "The marvels of Industry did not awe him, the progress of humanity he did not place in the triumph of matter in his eyes a man was a man only on condition of being a tabernacle of the living God."—"Wylie's Carlyle," chap. 24.

Carlyle's Religious Idealism is now found confronted by a "mechanical age;" an age swayed by a sort of spiritual and physical machine; an age, which suffers from the fact that its noble impulses are no longer brought out with freedom, naturally and unconsciously, without regard to consequences and criticism, but rather reach forward toward an independent and imagined end; not to that one end, which for Carlyle is the only one, the kingdom of God on Earth.

That Carlyle, although perhaps too inexorable in his antagonism to mechanical things, is not blind to the results which the progress in technical and other sciences has wrought for mankind, cannot be denied; nevertheless he believed

his chief mission to be in mercilessly attacking
the experiments of the mechanical mind in daring to interfere with fields with which it has no
concern ; viz., the fields of a higher, spiritual and
moral life, and, above all, in the field of Religion. . . . . In theology, philosophy and
pedagogy, as in all the sciences and arts, he
sees the pernicious increase of a mechanical
view of life.

"Thus we have machines for Education ; Lan-
castrian machines ; Hamiltonian machines ; mon-
itors, etc. Instruction, that mysterious commun-
ing of Wisdom with Ignorance, is no longer an
indefinable tentative process, requiring a study
of individual aptitudes, and a perpetual variation
of means and methods, to attain the same end ;
but a secure, universal, straight-forward business,
to be conducted in the gross by proper mechanism, with such intellect as comes to hand. Then
we have Religious machines; of all imaginable
varieties; the Bible-Society, professing a far
higher and heavenly structure, is found, on inquiry, to be altogether an earthly contrivance ;
supported by collection of moneys, by fomenting
of vanities, by puffing, by intrigue and chicane ;
a machine for converting the Heathen. It is the
same in all other departments. Has any man, or
any society of men a truth to speak, a piece of

spiritual work to do, they can no wise proceed
at once and with the mere natural organs, but
must first call a public meeting, appoint com-
mittees, issue prospectuses, eat a public dinner." *

"With individuals, in like manner, natural
strength avails little. No individual now hopes
to accomplish the poorest enterprise single-handed
and without mechanical aids. He must make interest with some existing corporation, and till his
fields with their oxen.

"In these days, more emphatically than ever,
'to live, signifies to unite with a party, or to
make one.' Philosophy, Science, Art, Literature,
all depend on machinery. No Newton, by silent
meditation, now discovers the System of the World
from the falling of an apple; but some quite other
than Newton stands in his Museum, his Scientific
Institution, and behind whole batteries of retorts,
digestors and galvanic piles imperatively 'interro-
gates Nature,'—w¹ ɔ, however, shows no haste to
answer. In defect of Raphaels, and Angelos, and
Mozarts, we have Royal Academies of Painting,
Sculpture, Music; whereby the languishing Spirit
of Art may be strengthened, as by the more generous diet of a Public Kitchen. Literature, too,
has its Paternoster-row of mechanism, its Trade

* Essay on Signs of the Times, p. 234.

dinners, its Editorial conclaves, and huge sub-
terranean, puffing bellows; so that books are not
only printed, but in a great measure written and
sold by machinery. . . . . Men are grown
mechanical in head and in heart, as well as in
hand. They have lost faith in individual endeavour, and in natural force of any kind. Not for
internal perfection, but for external combinations
and arrangements, for institutions, constitutions,—
for Mechanism of one sort or other, do they hope
and struggle." *

In what follows an attempt will be made to give
an idea of Carlyle's position with reference to the
several departments of spiritual life, which, under
the influence of Mechanism, have more or less
suffered.

---

* Essay on Signs of the Times, pp. 235-236.

CHAPTER III.

CARLYLE'S RELATION TO CHRISTI-ANITY.

1.—HIS VIEWS ON THE PERSONALITY OF CHRIST.
2.—HIS APPREHENSION OF THE SIGNIFICANCE OF CHRISTIANITY IN THE WORLD'S HISTORY.
3.—HIS NOTION OF THE NATURE OF CHRISTIANITY.

"To begin with our highest Spiritual function, with Religion," says Carlyle, "we might ask, Whither has Religion now fled? Of churches and their establishments we here say nothing; nor of the unhappy domains of Unbelief, and how innumerable men, blinded in their minds, have grown to live without God in the world; but, taking the fairest side of the matter, we ask, What is the nature of that same Religion, which still lingers in the hearts of the few, who are called, and call themselves, specially the Religious? Is it a healthy religion, vital, unconscious of itself; that shines forth spontaneously in doing of the Work, or even in preaching of the Word? Un-

happily, No. Instead of heroic martyr Conduct,
and inspired and soul-inspiring Eloquence, whereby Religion itself were brought home to our living
bosoms, to live and reign there, we have ' Dis-
cources on the Evidences,' endeavouring, with
small results, to make it probable that such a
thing as Religion exists. The most enthusiastic
Evangelicals do not preach a Gospel, but keep
describing how it should and might be preached.
To awaken the sacred fire of faith, as by a sacred
contagion, is not their endeavour, but, at most,
to describe how Faith shows and acts, and scientifically distinguish true Faith from false.   Religion, like all else, is conscious of itself, listens
to itself; it becomes less and less creative, vital;
more and more mechanical.   Considered as a
whole, the Christian Religion of late years has
been continually dissipating itself into Metaphysics; and threatens now to disappear, as some
rivers do in deserts of barren sand." *

The preceding words have already suggested
from what quarter Carlyle's position with reference
to Christianity may be expected. .

We shall next consider his position as to the
personality of Christ and the historical significance of Christianity.

---

* Characteristics, p. 20.

When Goethe on the 11th of March, 1832 (Eckerm, iii., 255) gives utterance to the following sentiment: "I consider the Gospels entirely genuine, for there is in them an image of a powerful grandeur which proceeds from the person of Christ and in so godlike a manner as only upon earth the Godlike has been revealed. If one asks me whether it may be in my nature to feel reverence and devotion to him, I answer, to be sure. I bow before him as before the highest revelation, the highest principle of morality," and when on the same day he says, "may spiritual culture advance, may the natural sciences grow broader and deeper, and the human spirit expand as it will, it will never be surpassed by the grandeur and moral development of Christianity as it glistens and sparkles in the Gospels;" and when Goethe crowns these expressions with the words, "We shall all of us come gradually out of a Christianity of words and belief to a Christianity of principle and action," it is in order that Carlyle's own conviction of the worth and the significance of the future of Christianity may also find expression. Carlyle's religious feeling became completely imbued with the teaching and character of Christ.

Carlyle never spoke a word which permitted of a double meaning, which did not show the com-

plete conviction of his heart, and in the following
plain language he expresses his belief in Christ:
"Highest of all Symbols are those wherein the
Artist or Poet has risen into Prophet, and all men
can recognise a present God and worship the
same. . . . Various enough have been such
religious Symbols, what we call *Religious;* as men
stood in this stage of culture or the other, and
could worse or better body-forth the Godlike:
some Symbols with a transient intrinsic worth;
many with only an extrinsic. If thou ask to what
height man has carried it in this manner, look
on one divinest Symbol: on Jesus of Nazareth,
and his Life, and his Biography, and what followed therefrom. Higher has the human Thought
not yet reached; This is Christianity and Christ-
endom, a Symbol of quite perennial, infinite
character; whose significance will ever demand
to be anew inquired into, and anew made manifest." *

"Small it is that thou canst trample the Earth
under thy feet, as old Greek Zeno trained thee:
thou canst love the Earth while it injures thee,
and even because it injures thee; for this a
Greater than Zeno was needed, and he, too, was
sent. Knowest thou that 'Worship of Sorrow?'

---

* Sartor Resartus, p. 155.

The Temple thereof, founded some eighteen centuries ago, now lies in ruins, overgrown with
jungle, the habitation of doleful creatures: nevertheless, venture forward; in a low crypt, arched
out of falling fragments, thou findest the Altar
still there, and its sacred Lamp perennially burning." *

The essence of the Christian doctrine for Carlyle is raised above all doubt and every logical
proof, it is implanted in every human heart, and
whether "in the believing or unbelieving mind,
must ever be regarded as the crowning glory, or
rather the life and soul, of our whole modern
culture!" †

And just for this reason Carlyle never became
tired of pointing out the untenableness of even
the most earnest essays to defend or assault the
Christian doctrine with the help of logic.

In his Essay on Voltaire we find these words:
"That the Christian Religion could have any
deeper foundation than Books, could possibly be
written in the purest nature of man, in mysterious, ineffaceable characters, to which Books, and
all Revelations and authentic traditions, were but
a subsidiary matter, were but as the *light* whereby that divine *writing* was to be read;—nothing

* Sartor Resartus, p. 133.
† Signs of the Times, p 242.

of this seems, even in the faintest manner, to
have occurred to Voltaire. Yet, herein, as we
believe that the whole world has now begun to
discover, lies the real essence of the question;
by the negative or affirmative decision of which,
the Christian Religion, anything that is worth
calling by that name, must fall, or endure forever.
We believe, also, that the wiser minds of our
age have already come to agreement in this question; or rather never were divided regarding it.
Christianity, the 'Worship of Sorrow,' has been
recognised as divine, on far other grounds than
'Essays on Miracles,' and by consideration infinitely deeper than would avail in any mere
'trial by jury.' He who argues against it, or for
it, in this manner, may be regarded as mistak-
ing its nature.* . . . . Our fathers were
wiser than we, when they said, in the deepest
seriousness, what we often hear in shallow mockery, that Religion is 'not of Sense, but of Faith;'
not of Understanding, but of Reason. He who
finds himself without the latter, who by all his
studying has failed to unfold it in himself, may
have studied to great or little purpose, we say
not which; but of the Christian Religion, as of
many other things, he has and can have no

---

* Essay on Voltaire, p. 172.

knowledge. The Christian Doctrine we often
hear likened to the Greek Philosophy, and found,
on all hands, some measurable way superior to
it : but this also seems a mistake. The Christian
Doctrine, that Doctrine of Humanity, in all senses
Godlike, and the parent of all Godlike virtues,
is not superior, or inferior, or equal, to any doctrine of Socrates or Thales; being of a totally
different nature ; differing from these, as a perfect Ideal Poem does from a correct Computation
in Arithmetic. He who compares it with such
standards may lament that, beyond the mere letter, the purport of this divine Humility has
never been disclosed to him; that the loftiest
feeling hitherto vouchsafed to mankind is yet
hidden from his eyes. * . . . . We understand ourselves to be risking no new assertion,
but simply repeating what is already the conviction of the greatest of our age, when we say,—
that cheerfully recognising, gratefully appropri-
ating whatever Voltaire has proved, or any other
man has proved, or shall prove, the Christian
Religion, once here, cannot again pass away;
that in one or the other form, it will endure
through all time; that as in Scripture, so also
in the heart of man, is written, ' the Gates of Hell

---

* Voltaire, p. 173.

shall not prevail against it.' Were the meaning of this Faith never so obscured, as, indeed, in all times, the coarse passions and perceptions of the world do all but obliterate it in the hearts of most; yet in every pure soul, in every Poet and Wise Man, it finds a new Missionary, a new Martyr, till the great volume of Universal History is finally closed, and man's destinies are fulfilled in this earth. 'It is a height to which the human species were fated and enabled to attain; and from which, having once retained it, they can never retrograde." *

These views of the historical significance of Christianity are almost identical with Goethe's; but as to the nature of Christianity itself, the two men take widely divergent paths.

" Christianity as 'the religion of expiation' has two poles, between which all Christian life oscillates: the one, negative, is the consciousness of sin, or of a contrast between God and man; the other, the positive pole, is the consciousness of grace, or of the annulling of that contrast, of the reconcilement of the disunited, and the reunion of God and man. According to the diversity in natures, the attractive power of Christianity rests now upon the side of

* Essay on Voltaire, pp. 172–174.

the negative and now upon that of the positive
pole." *

If we apply this idea to Carlyle, we come to
the conclusion that with him, exactly as with
Kant, Calvin, Knox, Cromwell, and all other men
who have grown up under the influence of defined notions of the Scotch Presbyterian Church,
sympathy is found to be more on the side of the
negative pole—decidedly in contrast to Goethe.

The extent of the preponderating notions as
to sinfulness and the imperfectness of human
nature induced Carlyle to take this position—
perhaps already well grounded in ˙his nature,˙
at all events, further developed by education.

Here views inherited from his ancestors suddenly stand out in rugged contrast to the Religious Idealism of his soul, and here lies darkly
and mysteriously the essence of the contradiction of his religious views so enigmatically split
asunder.

Carlyle, whom we even now hear saying: Man
is a divine mystery, every man has an immortal
soul which is the mirror and living reflection
of God ; Carlyle, whose gentle soul fully coincides
with the belief that an infinite and powerful Good

* These words, taken from a paper of Otto Pfleiderer's on
"Goethe's Conception of Religion," are to be found in the
"Protestantische Kirchenzeitung," April 11, 1883.

exists, a God, to whom every man's well being
and perfection lies near, who, as the "Omnipo-
tent" and the "All-Good" is able to find ways
and means to advance the perfection of every
man, to purify every man; Carlyle, when he steps
forth as "admonisher," and tries to show the
absolute necessity of the morality of the world
with firo and sword—as he has himself con-
fessed—has gone hand in hand with Calvinism
in the question of Predestination.

And though this conviction as to the possibility of the complete damnation of mankind—
in the Dantean sense—did not cause him to become a pessimist (what the logical result of it
would have been), as a result of it, his religious
views were always tinged with a sort of melancholy, dejection and sadness which shows a pro-
digious digression from Goethe's religious views.
"Religion contains an infinite amount of sadness,"—this sentence of Novalis' comes directly
from his heart. The religion of sadness, the religion of suffering, is his constantly recurring
definition of Christianity. Goethe's expression,
"the sanctuary of pain" he admitted completely
into his realm of ideas and quoted it repeatedly.

To be sure, we often find in his Journal such
expressions as the following: "I say to myself,
why shouldst thou not be thankful? God is

good, all this life is a heavenly miracle, great,
though stern and sad." "The universe is full
of love, but also of inexorable sternness and
severity, and it remains for ever true that God
reigns."

But the grim sternness and the inexorable harsh-
ness which the ever insufficient nature of man
brings with it, appears always like a ghost between him and God, and robs him—at least at
times—of the content of his own soul.

"I, like all mortals, have to feel the inexorable
that there is in life, and to say, as piously as
I can: God's will, God's will!" . . . "*Sunt
lacrimæ rerum! Fractus bello, fessus annis*," he
writes. "The deepest De Profundis was trifling
in comparison with the feelings in my heart.
There is nothing but wail and lamentation in the
heart of all my thoughts." "I am very wae and
lonely here," he writes to his wife, "take care,
take care of thy poor little self, for truly enough,
I have no other!" "A solemn kind of sadness,
a gloom of mind which, though heavy to bear,
is not unallied with sacredness and blessedness."
"There is nothing of joyful in my life, nor ever
likely to be; no truly loved or loving soul—or
practically as good as none—left to me in the
earth any more. The one object that is wholly
beautiful and noble, and in any sort helpful to

my poor heart, is she whom I do not name. The thought of her is drowned in sorrow to me, but also in tenderness, in love inexpressible." *

A deep insight into his life is given in a letter written on June 12, 1847, to the excellent Thomas Erskine, of Linlathen : " One is warned by Nature herself not to 'sit down by the side of sad thoughts,' as my friend Oliver has it, and dwell voluntarily with what is sorrowful and painful. Yet at the same time one has to say for one's self—at least I have—that all the *good* I ever got, came to me rather in the shape of sorrow : that there is nothing noble or godlike in the world but has in it something of ' infinite sadness,' very different indeed from what the current moral philosophies represent to us." †

This shows the seriousness, the sadness and melancholy with which his whole thought is penetrated. It is the rebound of his soul, and of the infinite suffering with which his life is filled. The single hidden reason for all this appears to lie in the much too tender nature of his heart, which is always being wounded, even in his love for his wife—and furthermore in the peculiar excitability of his nature. His wife

* Journal, Sep. 30, 1867.
† Froude's Life of Carlyle, Franklin Square Ed., vol. ii., p. 6.

was once taken when she was very ill to the baths at St. Leonards, while he himself was returning to his work in London, and when the sufferer was somewhat better, he writes, on September 29th, 1864, in answer to a letter from her:

"Oh, my suffering little Jeannie! Not a wink of real sleep again for you. I read (your letter) with that kind of heart you may suppose in the bright beautiful morning. And yet, dearest, there is something in your note that is welcomer to me than anything I have yet had—a sound of *piety*, of devout humiliation and gentle hope, and submission to the Highest, which affects me much and has been a great comfort for me. Yes, poor darling! This was wanted. Proud stoicism you never failed in, nor do I want you to abate of it. But there is something beyond of which I believe you have had too little. It softens the angry heart and is far from weakening it—nay, is the final strength of it, the fountain and nourishment of all real strength. Come home to your own poor nest again. . . . . We have had a great deal of hard travelling together, we will not break down yet, please God."

This letter fits completely into this connection. It shows what his real trouble was; what oppressed him; what made him unhappy; what filled his whole life with gloom and sadness, and

what a sombre veil beclouded his religion. All
of which, however beautiful the picture that produces this " ascetic pessimistic " aspect of Christianity, actually interfered with his keeping a
strong grasp on that joyous, sunny height of
Goethe's standpoint, whose " preëminently happy
spirit," conscious of moral greatness, willingly admits "man's hereditary shortcomings," but without
laying special stress upon this, and being completely lifted above sorrow and sin, soars to that
"sublime view of the world," where satisfaction,
in the bitterest suffering itself, consists in "recognising God," no matter how and where He may
reveal himself.   That is the actual blessedness on
Earth.

> " Were not the eye so luminous,
>   How could it ever see the sun?
>   Lived not in us God's influence,
>   How could the divine delight us?" *

This is Goethe's unflinching belief in the divine
nature of man, a belief which could never in any
way be affected by the gloomy influence of the
doctrine of predestination.   It was this belief
in the " natural holiness of human nature " that
separated Goethe, once for all, from the followers
of the Augustinian doctrines, Luther himself in-

---

* Goethe, Sprüche in Prosa, p. 120.   Ed. Leoper.

cluded, and led him to the party of Pelagius. It
was as he himself called it, "Christianity for his
own private use." *

If with Goethe this free and joyous contempla-
tion of life, in strong contrast to the gloomy and
untrue teachings of the extreme insufficiency of
human nature, was always able to win the victory, it was—however obstructed by gloomy views—
fundamentally the same as that of Carlyle.

The optimistic and religious Idealism took possession of his soul, just as it does in the case
of every healthy man's, and it was constantly
brought home to him that "the gate of Hell shall
have no strength."

He cries out: "The Earth is not—in the name
of God—a place of bitter hopelessness for any
living creature, but it is emphatically the place of
hope for all." †

"One asks, Is man alone born to sorrow that
has neither healing nor blessedness in it? All
nature, from all corners, answers, No—for all
the wise, No.   Only _Yea_ for the unwise, who
have man's susceptibilities, appetites, capabilities,
and not the insights and rugged virtues of men." ‡

"Yes, the Redeemer liveth.   He is no Jew, or

---

* Wahrheit und Dichtung, (Hempel) vol. iii, p. 178.
† Froude's Life of Carlyle, vol. iii., p. 15.
‡ Op. cit., p. 42.

image of a man, or surplice, or old creed, but
the Unnamable Maker of us, voiceless, formless
within our own soul, whose voice *is* every noble
and genuine impulse of our souls. He is yet
there, in us and around us, and *we* are there.
No Eremite or fanatic whatever had more than
we have; how much less had most of them?"

Carlyle's Calvinistic views stand not altogether
in inexplicable contradiction to this sentiment.
What induced him to doubt of the insufficiency
of human nature—divine as it is and should be—
what led him to a complete and exaggerated
contempt for the world, was his unrelenting hate
of the evil, and the immoral as it exists, as a
rather large factor in the world's history. This
is a point which properly belongs to the Chapter
on Ethics, but must, nevertheless, be discussed
here, where he defines his position as to Predestination and Christianity in general.

The moral duty imposed upon us by God,
whose fulfillment—as Carlyle has already said—
is our divine *right*, will only be recognized by
a few, and performed by still fewer. Only the
soul of a hero can perform it—a man of extraordinary greatness and mellowness—a man chosen
by God; average humanity deprives itself of this
heroism; does not listen to the voice of its heart,
which is the command of God; and so misses

its divine call. And as the noble man can only hate and despise what is worthless, so does also the righteous God. That the just God judges according to a higher law than that of human morality, that with him it is the law of love which judges, finds in Carlyle no fixed abode. Where the question is one of the practical furtherance of morality, Carlyle comes out strongly as "admonisher." Here—and here only—is Carlyle's God found. The Old Testament God, the punishing and revengeful God is his, and his religion might be said to be that of "Job, Isaiah and Ezekiel." His bosom is filled with hatred and revenge toward the unworthy. The Christian doctrine of forgiveness and of human love recedes, and Hell opens her gates for the wicked who have devoted themselves voluntarily to destruction, and with whom God and Eternity can have nothing in common.

At this point Carlyle returns to the doctrines of the Church, but fails to reach the heights which the Christianity of Goethe and Schiller embraced. Carlyle forgets the words:

> "All sins shall be forgiven,
> And Hell shall no more be."

One can see from these views of the justice of the punishing God, how Carlyle clung to the ascetic-pessimistic aspect of Christianity; how it was that the idea of mercy and of love—which, placed above everything else, even justice itself, and finally carrying victory with it—was always receding with him, and especially when it comes to the point of inciting to morality the degenerated elements of the world.

That these gloomy views do not play an important role with Carlyle; that the "religion of expiation," in its chief significance as a mercy bringer, finds an explanation in him, remains in spite of everything, a determined fact, though Carlyle as a "prophet" and preacher (and that he considered was his mission in life) did not recognize the "unrestricted" free and "joyful Godliness" acknowledged by Goethe as the final goal. Carlyle had not studied in the school of antiquity as had Goethe.   For his own inner experience there was no morality which had not been won by severe battles; no morality which, as a free gift of Nature, is given to man in his cradle. Carlyle's birth, his education, his whole nature had denied him "the hopeful and happy spirit"— which, however, would not have been necessary to assist him to conquer the passionate battles against immorality. That, however, the "Sinai's thunder" of the punishing God did not indicate his latest views on this subject cannot be too earnestly emphasized.

"Can thunder from all the thirty-two azimuths, repeated daily for centuries of years, make God's Laws more godlike to me? Brother, No. Perhaps I am grown to be a man now; and do not need the thunder and the terror any longer! Perhaps I am above being frightened; perhaps it is not Fear, but Reverence alone, that shall now lead me! Revelations, Inspirations? Yes; and thy own god-created Soul; dost thou not call that a 'revelation?' Who made *Thee?* Where didst Thou come from? The voice of Eternity, if thou be not a blasphemer and poor asphyxiated mute, speaks with that tongue of thine! *Thou* art the latest Birth of Nature; it is 'the Inspiration of the Almighty' that giveth *thee* understanding! My brother, my brother!" *

---

* Past and Present, p. 198.

CHAPTER IV.

CARLYLE AND THE VARIOUS PHASES OF CHRISTIANITY: THE CHURCH AND THEOLOGICAL SCIENCE.

Motto: "Intolerance, animosity can forward no cause, and least of all becomes the cause of moral and religious truth. A wise man has well reminded us 'that in any controversy the moment we feel angry we have already ceased striving for Truth, and begun striving for ourselves.' "—Carlyle's Essay on Voltaire, p. 181.

On October 11th, 1841, Carlyle writes to the excellent and great Scotch divine, Chalmers: "that you, with your generous, hopeful heart, believe that there may still exist in our actual churches enough of divine fire to awaken the supine rich and the degraded poor, and act victoriously against such a mass of pressing and ever-accumulating evils—alas! what worse could be said of this by the bitterest opponent of it, than that it is a noble hoping against hope, a noble strenuous determination to gather from the

dry deciduous tree what the green alone could
yield." *

Carlyle was not a bitter enemy to "the church"
as he has frequently been represented in England.
He was of the deepest conviction that all mankind belong to one universal divine fellowship,
which, independent of churches, ceremonies and
liturgies, rests only and solely in the heart of
man. He was an enemy to falsehood and to
hypocritical intolerance; and where, indeed, is
this more to be found in the world's history than
in priestcraft?

His relation to the Church again is not essentially different from Goethe's.

In his youth he attended the Scotch Presbyterian Church, but later in life his experience
was similar to Goethe's. The mere externali-
ties of the Church, its accepted dogmas re-
pelled him. Carlyle was all his life of a pious
frame of mind, and was able to enter into the
feelings of the pious reverence of the savage
before his fetish, and of the heathen before his
idol. The sight of a fervently praying woman
in the cathedral at Brügge filled him with melancholy —" a more beautiful picture than all the
pictures of Rubens and Rembrandt." He could

---

* Life of Chalmers (Hanna) p. 109.

thoroughly understand that inner need—what it is that impels a devout Catholic to long for the mediation of a saint; but all forms and empty creeds, or creeds whose meaning he—after sincere trial—could not comprehend, filled him with the same feeling as the dull belief of a sceptic did—with horror and compassion. Like Goethe, he remained true to the Bible during his whole life: in Craigenputtock he read aloud from it for morning prayers. "In the poorest cottage," he says in 1832, "is one Book, wherein for several thousands of years, the spirit of man has found light, and nourishment, and an interpreting response to whatever is Deepest in him; wherein still, to this day, for the eye that will look well, the mystery of Existence reflects itself, if not resolved, yet revealed, and prophetically emblemed," and again in 1867 he calls the Bible "the truest of all books," * as earlier, in 1850, he had alluded to it as "the most earnest of books," † and it was to the end of his life—as well as Goethe and Shakespeare—his faithful companion. ‡ That he recognized, as Goethe did, that there were other revelations, we see from the following: "One

---

* Shooting Niagara, p. 221.
† Latter-Day Pamphlets, p. 274.
‡ Froude's Life of Carlyle, vol. iv., chap. 24.

Bible I know, of whose Plenary Inspiration doubt
is not so much as possible; nay, with my own
eyes I saw the God's-Hand writing it; thereof
all other Bibles are but Leaves,—say, in Picture-
Writing to assist the weaker faculty." *

Goethe writes to Lavater, August 9th, 1782,
"You consider the Gospel as it stands divine
Truth. A distinct voice from Heaven would not
convince me that water burns and fire quenches,
that birth may be miraculous, and that a dead
person is raised to life; far more do I consider
all this blasphemy against the great God and his
revelations in Nature. You find nothing more
beautiful than the Gospels; I find a thousand
written pages by ancients and moderns just as
beautiful and useful and indispensible to humanity."

These words describe Carlyle's position per-
fectly. "Art thou a grown baby, then, to fancy
that the miracle lies in miles of distance, or in
pounds of avoirdupois; and not to see that
the true inexplicable God-revealing miracle lies
in this, that I can stretch forth my hand at
all; that I have free Force to clutch aught
therewith ? " † Man is a great miracle, sufficient-

* Sartor Resartus, p. 134.
† Op. cit., p. 182.

ly inexplicable, so that others are entirely super-
fluous. Things were regarded by many men as
miracles which were simply incredible, and which
could not be supported or made credible by logic
or "metaphysical hocus-pocus" or "theosophical
moonshine."

When such ceremonies as baptism throw Goethe
so out of tune that he cannot be present at them;
when in Meiningen he is displeased because his
residence is opposite a church, and he writes on
May 12th, 1782, to Frau von Stein: "Here I
live opposite a church, which is a terrible situa-
tion for one who neither prays upon this or that
mountain, and has no prescribed hours to worship God;" and when Schiller frankly declares
that "no sermon precisely pleases him," it is
exactly what we often meet with in Carlyle's Journal and works.

Nevertheless, in the beginning of his London
life, he made an attempt to identify himself with
some church, but in vain. "I tried various chap-
els; I found in each some vulgar, illiterate man
declaiming about matters of which he knew nothing. I tried the Church of England. I found
there a decent educated gentleman reading out
of a book words very beautiful, which had expressed once the serious thoughts of pious, admirable souls. I decidedly preferred the Church

of England man; but I had to say to him: 'I perceive, sir, that at the bottom you know as little about the matter as the other fellow.'"*

"It is every way strange to consider," he once wrote, "what Christianity, so-called, has grown to within these two centuries—on the Howard and Fry side as on every other—a paltry, mealy-mouthed 'religion of cowards,' which also, as I believe, awaits its 'abolition' from the avenging power. If men will turn away their faces from God and set up idols, temporary phantasms, instead of the Eternal One—alas! the consequences are from of old well known." †

Carlyle's position as to the Church on the one hand, and dogmatic theological science on the other, finds an explanation in his comprehension of the idea of God.

When Sterling took exception to Professor Teufelsdröckh's God because it appeared to be "no personal God," Carlyle replied: "A grave charge, nevertheless—an awful charge—to which, if I mistake not, the Professor, laying his hand on his heart, will reply with some gesture expressing the solemnest *denial*. In gesture rather than in speech, for the *Highest cannot* be spoken

---

* Froude's Life of Carlyle, vol. iii., p. 10.
† Op. cit., vol. iv., p. 6.

in words. Personal! Impersonal! Me! Thou!
What meaning can any mortal (after all) attach
to them in reference to *such* an object? *Wer
darf Ihn nennen?* I dare not and do not. That
you dare and do (to some greater extent) is a
matter I am far from taking offence at. Nay,
with all sincerity, I can rejoice that you have
a creed of that kind which gives you happy
thoughts, nerves you for good actions, brings
you into readier communion with many good
men. My true wish is, that such a creed may
long hold compactly together in you, and be 'a
covert from the heat, a shelter from the storm,
as the shadow of a great rock in a weary land.'
Well is it, if we have a printed litany to pray
from; and yet not *ill* if we *can* pray in *silence;*
for silence, too, is audible *there*. Finally, assume
yourself that I am neither Pagan nor Turk, nor
circumcised Jew, but an unfortunate Christian
individual resident at Chelsea in *this* year of
grace, neither Pantheist, nor Pot-theist, nor any
Theist or Ist whatsoever, having the most decided contempt for all such manner of system-
builders or sect-founders—as far as contempt
may be compatible with so mild a nature—feeling well beforehand (taught by long experience)
that all such are and ever must be *wrong*. By
God's blessing, one has got two eyes to look

with, also a mind capable of knowing, of believing. This is all the creed I will at this time insist on. And now may I beg one thing, that whenever in my thoughts or your own, you fall on any dogma that tends to estrange you from me, pray believe *that* to be *false*, false as Beelzebub, till you get clearer evidence." *

The preceding words clearly show the bent of Carlyle's mind towards religious matters. As he himself was continually saying with severeness, "creeds the recital of certain ceremonies," "the thirty-nine articles," rituals and liturgies, hierarchies, and catechisms have nothing whatever to do with the nature of belief itself, with religion itself, for "religion is no mere external appendage;" those things are only the outer husk, those same church clothes "have gone sorrowfully out-at-elbows;" first must the dead letter of religion own itself dead, if the living spirit of religion is to arise on us, "newborn of Heaven." †

Religion is the heavenly light which slumbers in the soul of man. ‡ It is the great, heavenly divine truth which has been left to us as a joy, a comfort, and a protection in the midst of the

* Froude's Life of Carlyle, vol. iii., p. 10.
† Sartor Resartus, bk. ii., chap. 3.
‡ Latter-Day Pamphlets, p. 195.

changeful cycles of the world; it is an eternal
truth which we can never question, "it does not
consist in the many things which man is in doubt
of and tries to believe, but of the few he is assured
of, and has no need of effort for believing."

Therefore it is vain, impossible, and for the
weak mind it is even dangerous and injurious to
attempt to prove the necessity, the possibility of
religion according to a metaphysical method; it
is impossible, because religion is not a thing of
logical or mathematical understanding, but of the
human, feeling heart, of living belief. "An amal-
gam of Christian verities" and modern critical
philosophy was and could be nothing else but
"poisonous insincerity." * But this subject is
well treated in Carlyle's Life of Sterling.

There is found a delicately executed picture of
the earnest and true endeavour of John Sterling
to bring theology into harmony and relation with
the critical philosophy of Kant—according to
Coleridge's example—and of the disastrous effect
of this endeavour upon a true and frank nature.

"No man of Sterling's veracity, had he clearly
consulted his own heart, or had his own heart
been capable of clearly responding, and not been
dazzled and bewildered by transient phantasies

---

* Froude's Life of Carlyle, vol. iii., chap. 2.

and theosophic moonshine—could have under-
taken this function. His heart would have an-
swered: 'No, thou canst not.' 'What is incredible to thee, thou shalt not, at thy soul's
peril, attempt to believe!' Else whither for a
refuge, or die here. Go to Perdition if thou
must,—but not with a lie in thy mouth; by
the Eternal Maker, no!" *

"Concerning this attempt of Sterling's to find
sanctuary in the old Church, and desperately
grasp the hem of her garment in such manner,
there will at present be many opinions: and mine
must be recorded here in flat reproval of it, in
mere pitying condemnation of it, as a rash, false,
unwise and unpermitted step. . . . . Alas,
if we did remember the divine and awful nature
of God's Truth, and had not so forgotten it as
poor doomed creatures never did before,—should
we, durst we, in our most audacious moments,
think of wedding it to the world's Untruth, which
is also, like all untruths, the Devil's? Only in
in the world's last lethargy can such things be
done, and accounted safe and pious! Fools!
'Do you think the living God is a buzzard idol,'
sternly asks Milton, 'that you dare address Him
in this manner?' Such darkness, thick sluggish

* Carlyle's Life of Sterling, chap. 2.

clouds of cowardice and oblivious baseness, have accumulated on us: thickening as if towards the eternal sleep! It is not now known, what never needed proof or statement before, that Religion is not a doubt; that it is a certainty,—or else a mockery and horror. That none or all of the many things we are in doubt about, and need to have demonstrated and rendered probable, can, by any alchymy be made a 'Religion' for us; but are and must continue a baleful, quiet or unquiet Hypocrisy for us; and bring—*salvation*, do we fancy? I think, it is another thing they will bring, and are on all hands, visibly bringing, this good while!" *

In the same text is found Carlyle's terrible castigatory sermon against the Jesuits:

"Man's religion, whatever it may be, is a discerned fact, and coherent system of discerned facts; he stands fronting the worlds and eternities upon it. to *doubt* of it is not permissible at all! He must verify or expel his doubts, convert them into certainty of Yes or No; or they will be the death of his religion. But, on the other hand, convert them into certainty of Yes *and* No; or even of Yes *though* No, as the Ignatian method is, what will become of your religion? . . . .

---

* Carlyle's Life of Sterling, Part I., chap. 15.

The religion of a man in these strange circumstances, what living conviction he has about his Destiny in this Universe, falls into a most strange condition;—and, in truth, I have observed, is apt to take refuge in the stomach mainly. The man goes through his prescribed fugle-motions at church and elsewhere, keeping his conscience and sense of decency at ease thereby; and in some empty part of his brain, if he have fancy left, or brain other than a beaver's, there goes on occasionally some dance of dreamy hypotheses, sentimental echoes, shadows, and other inane make-believes,—which I think are quite the contrary of a possession to him; leading to no clear Faith, or divine life-and-death Certainty of any kind; but to a torpid species of *delirium somnians* and *delirium stertens* rather. In his head or in his heart this man has of available religion none." *

The Pig Philosophy is the result of such manœuvring.

If Carlyle ever touches upon this subject, he takes especial pains to censure Coleridge's course, in which more or less successful and excellent men, such as Maurice, Kingsley, Hare and Sterling, have sought their happiness; but the true

* Latter-Day Pamphlets, p. 267.

kernel, Coleridge's honest effort, he by no means misconceived.

"Let me not be unjust to this memorable man," he says. "Surely there was here, in his pious, ever-labouring, subtle mind, a precious truth, or prefigurement of truth; and yet a fatal delusion withal. Prefigurement that, in spite of beaver sciences and temporary spiritual hebetude and cecity, man and his Universe were eternally divine; and that no past nobleness, or revelation of the divine, could or would ever be lost to him. Most true, surely, and worthy of all acceptance. Good also to do what you can with old Churches and practical Symbols of the Noble: nay, quit not the burnt ruins of them while you find there is still gold to be dug there. But, on the whole, do not think you can, by logical alchymy, distil astral spirits from them; or, if you could, that said astral spirits, or defunct logical phantasms, could serve you in anything. What the light of your mind, which is the direct inspiration of the Almighty, pronounces incredible,—that, in God's name, leave uncredited; at your peril do not try believing that. No subtlest hocus-pocus of 'reason' *versus* 'understanding' will avail for that feat,—and it is terribly perilous to try it in these provinces!" *

---
* Carlyle's Life of Sterling, p. 53.

The same thought is expressed in a letter written to Sterling on June 7th, 1837 :

"You announce that you are rather quitting philosophy and theology—I predict that you will quit them more and more. I give it you as my decided prognosis that the two provinces in question are become theorem, brain-web and shadow, wherein no earnest soul can find solidity for itself. Shadow, I say; yet the shadow projected from an everlasting reality that is within ourselves. Quit the shadow. Seek the reality."

CHAPTER V.

GOD.

It may now be stated in a very few words what Carlyle regarded as the "truth."

No "new religion" need be looked for. "Simple souls still clamour occasionally for what they call a 'new religion.' My friends, you will not get this new religion of yours;—I perceive you already have it, always had it! All that is *true* is your 'religion,'—is it not? Commanded by the Eternal God to be *performed*, I should think, if it is true!

"Your way of looking at life has been at all times a mirror picture of mankind, and 'if you have now no Heaven to look to; if you now sprawl, lamed and lost, sunk to the chin in the pathless sloughs of this lower world without guidance from above, know that the fault is not Heaven's at all, but your own! . . . . Arise, make this thing more divine, and that thing,— and thyself, of all things; and work, and sleep not; for the night cometh, wherein no man can work!" *

"This new religion is no pill to be swallowed down—it is but a reawakening of thy own Self from within." † It must exert itself to obtain a true and warm belief in God and to reach moral activity. This new religion consists in the reconquered and resuscitated religious feeling of a change of heart. Therein lies the real salvation of the world.

"The Maker's Laws, whether they are promulgated in Sinai Thunder, to the ear or imagination, or quite otherwise promulgated, are the Laws of God; transcendant, everlasting, imperatively demanding obedience from all men. The Universe is made by Law; the great Soul of the World is just and not unjust. Look then, if thou have eyes or soul left, into this shoreless Incomprehensible: into the heart of its tumultuous Appearances, Embroilments, and mad Time-Vortexes, is there not, silent, eternal, an All-just, an All-beautiful; sole Reality and ultimate controlling power of the whole? This is not a figure of speech; this is a fact. The fact of Gravitation, known to all animals, is not surer than this

---

* Latter-Day Pamphlets, p. 285.
† Past and Present, p. 199.

inner Fact, which may be known to all men. He
who knows this, it will sink, silent, awful, unspeakable into his heart. He will say with
Faust: 'Who *dare* name Him?' Most rituals or
'namings' he will fall in with at present, are
like to be 'namings'—which shall be nameless!
In silence, in the Eternal Temple, let him worship, if there be no fit word. Such knowledge,
the crown of his whole spiritual being, the life
of his life, let him keep and sacredly walk by.
He has a religion. Hourly and daily, for himself and for the whole world, a faithful, un-
spoken, but not ineffectual prayer rises, 'Thy
will be done.' His whole work on Earth is an
emblematic spoken or acted prayer, Be the will
of God done on Earth,—not the Devil's will,
or any of the Devil's servant's wills! He has
a religion, this man; an everlasting Load-star
that beams the brighter in the Heavens, the
darker here on Earth grows the night around
him." *

To perform God's will, to live a pious life, that
is Carlyle's simple doctrine—whether the heart
feels happy in it or not, is not taken into consideration at all: man must keep God's com-
mandments, must be moral. And only so far as

---

* Carlyle's Past and Present, p. 197.

Christianity teaches this, only so far as the Christian is the most perfect ideal of a "moral Religion," does Carlyle feel respect for it. He has nothing whatever to do with "forms, rituals, creeds and ceremonies," as he himself always says. To use Fichte's words: "his religious ideas are not concerned with imputing qualities to God which are acknowledged, or should be acknowledged, as having no reference to our moral destiny."

CHAPTER VI.

CARLYLE'S ATTITUDE TOWARD SCIENCE, AND ESPECIALLY TOWARD PHILOSOPHY.

C'est d' Allemagne que Carlyle a tiré ses plus grand idées. Il y a étudié. . . . . De 1780 à 1830 l'Allemagne a produit toutes les idées de notre âge historique, et pendant un demi—siècle encore, pendant un siècle pent-être, notre grandes affaire sera de les repenser.—Taine, Idéalisme Anglais p. 72; also in his Lit. Hist., 5, 4, §2 1, p. 658. [English Translation.]

An irreverent knowledge is no knowledge.—Carlyle's Essay on Chartism, p. 178.

From Carlyle's deepest conviction that the—unconsciously living—religious feeling of veneration for the divine which is everywhere present, not only satisfies the highest moral needs, but actually constitutes the only highest development of mankind—is shown his attitude towards science in general, and philosophy in particular.

If the "philosophical-scientific tendency" of the times (as Fichte expresses it) is inclined "to grant nothing but what is comprehensible," and nothing but what the "carpenter's rule" can establish; if merely sensuous empiricism relies

on Science whose foundations are merely based
upon logical conclusions and deductions; if it
attempts to ignore or suppress the incomprehensible, the mysterious, the transcendental and the
metaphysical which represents the element of
religion; * or if it shows it to be absurd fanati-
cism or mysticism, with such a state of things
which Carlyle finds too widely spread throughout
the whole of English and French philosophy up
to his own time, he has absolutely no sympathy.

But he joyfully recognized the results and
ideals of the "real" philosophy which he believed was found in the efforts of the German
thinkers—whose early dawn for England he saw
coming from Dugald Steward.

According to Carlyle's conviction, an accurate
knowledge of the nature of philosophy and its
problems was first made possible in Germany by
the critical philosophy of Kant; its problems
which (according to Carlyle's comprehension), in
order that the inner eye of truth might be opened,
rested upon an indubitable principle, and the
acceptance of "the absolutely and primitively
True;" † rested upon the "primitively True"
which, as the beginning of all philosophy, is

---

* Fichte, 7, 241.
† Essay, State of General Literature.

written in the soul of man; rested upon that
truth which can never be uttered by philosophy
alone, whose existence philosophy herself will
never be able to prove, even with the help of logic
and science.

Carlyle awards to philosophy only a limited
province : he regards it only as a high and noble
means to a higher and nobler end ; to that higher
end which increases the view that " the belief in
Religion " for all men, as well as for thinkers
and philosophers, is the greatest gift that can
be bestowed—a gift which (according to his notion) is even again only a means to an end—that
of some living achievement.

To have raised this idea to a scientific fact was
the service which the Germans—in his eyes—
had rendered to mankind, and his attitude toward
philosophy is found everywhere in his judgments
of the several directions which the history of
philosophy has taken.

" In most of the European nations there is no
such thing as a Science of Mind ; only more or
less advancement in the general sciences or the
special sciences of matter. . . . . So it is
in France and in England, only the Germans
have made any decisive effort in 'psychological
science ;' the science of the age, in short, is
physical, chemical, physiological ; in all shapes

mechanical. Our favourite mathematics, the high-
ly prized exponent of all these sciences, has also
become more and more mechanical. Excellence
in the higher branches of mathematics depends
less on the natural genius than on acquired ex-
pertness in wielding its machinery. Without un-
dervaluing the wonderful results which a Le-
grange or a Laplace educes by means of it, we
may remark, that their calculus, differential and
integral, is little else than a more cunningly con-
structed arithmetical mill; when the factors being
put in, are, as it were, ground into the true
product, under cover, and without other effort on
our part than a steady turning of the handles.
We have more Mathematics than ever; but less
Mathesis. Archimedes and Plato could not have
read the *Méchanique Céleste;* but neither would
the whole French Institute see aught in the saying, ' God geometrises!' but a sentimental rodo-
montrade." *

Since Locke's time our whole metaphysics has
not been spiritual, but physical and material.
The unusual respect with which his Essay has
always been held (a respect founded upon the
excellent character of the man), is an extraordinary sign of the times. Its whole teaching, in

---

* Signs of the Times, pp. 236-237.

its methods and its results, is mechanical according to its aim and origin. It is no philosophy of the mind, only an examination of the origin of consciousness, of our ideas—or, as we might say, a history of their origin; what we may be able to see with the mind and in the mind; of the great mystery of our moral obligation and of our moral freedom; that restricted or unrestricted dependence of matter on mind; our mysterious conceptions of Time and Space; of God and the Universe never once are touched upon in all these examinations, and do not appear to have the least connection with the purport of the Essay.

The earliest form of Scotch metaphysics had an indistinct conception that this was false, but they did not, however, attempt to correct it. Reid's school had from the start taken a mechanical trend, as no other seemed to appear to them; the wonderful conclusions which Hume reached—starting from facts which had been accepted by Reid's School were founded by this same Scotch School. They let "instinct" loose, like a mastiff, in order to render their own position secure from the adversaries. They pull themselves merrily along—by the logical chains which Hume threw out to them and to the whole world—into the boundless abysses of Atheism and Fatalism.

But in some way the chain broke between them, and the end of the whole matter was that neither one grieved for the other—even as little as for the contemporary philosophical movement in England which was kept together by such men as Hartley, Darwin and Priestley. Hartley's "vibrations" and "vibratiuncles" were, one could easily believe, mechanical and material enough, but our neighbours on the Continent could go still farther.

One of her philosophers has made the extraordinary discovery that as the liver produces bile so the brain secretes thoughts; an astounding fact this, which Dr. Cabanis recently in his *Rapports du Physique et du Moral de l'homme* has followed to its extreme ends. The metaphysics of this searcher is, nevertheless, not shadowless and unsubstantial! With his operating knife and his "psychological sounding leads" he dissects the whole ethical structure of mankind, and then offers it to the thinking judgment of the world under a microscope, blowing it loud through his anatomical tube. Thought—he admits—is still secreted in the brain; but then, to be sure, one could consistently conclude—an interesting fact—that poetry and religion are both "product of the smaller intestines!"

We cherish the greatest admiration for this learned man; with what scientific Stoicism does he

not stride through the world of miracles without
being amazed; like a philosopher through an enor-
mous Vauxhall, whose fireworks and water-falls
and dashing music is the joy and delight of the
crowd, but for him nothing more than " saltpetre,
pasteboard and catgut." *

We conclude here Carlyle's animadversions on
the mechanical aspects of English and French
philosophers, and turn our attention to his judgment of those philosophies—especially the German critical philosophy—which makes an end
of " perversion of all philosophies."

" The Kantist, in direct contradiction to Locke
and all his followers, both of the French and
English or Scotch Schools, commences from within, and proceeds outwards; instead of commenc-
ing from without, and, with various precautions
and hesitations, endeavouring to proceed inwards.
The ultimate aim of all Philosophy must be to
interpret appearances,—from the given symbol
to ascertain the thing. Now the first step towards this, the aim of what may be called Primary or Critical Philosophy, must be to find
some indubitable principle; to fix ourselves on
some unchangeable basis; to discover what the
Germans call the *Urwahr*, the Primitive Truth,

---

* Essays, vol. ii., p, 238.

the necessarily, absolutely and eternally *True.*
This necessarily True, this absolute basis of
Truth, Locke silently, and Reid and his followers
with more tumult, find in a certain modified Experience, and evidence of Sense, in the universal
and natural persuasion of all men. Not so the
Germans: they deny that there is here any absolute Truth, or that any Philosophy whatever
can be built on such a basis; nay, they go to
the length of asserting, that such an appeal even
to the universal persuasions of mankind, gather
them with what precautions you may, amounts
to a total abdication of Philosophy, strictly so
called, and renders not only its farther progress,
but its very existence, impossible. What, they
would say, have the persuasions, or instinctive
beliefs, or whatever they are called, of men, to
do in this matter? Is it not the object of
Philosophy to enlighten, and rectify, and many
times directly contradict these very beliefs. . . .
The Germans take up this matter differently,
and would assail Hume, not in his outworks,
but in the centre of his citadel. They deny his
first principle, that Sense is the only inlet of
Knowledge, that Experience is the primary ground
of Belief. Their Primitive Truth, however, they
seek, not historically and by experiment, in the
univeral persuasions of men, but by intuition,

in the deepest and purest nature of Man. Instead of attempting, which they consider vain,
to prove the existence of God, Virtue, an im-
material Soul, by inferences drawn, as the conclusion of all Philosophy, from the world of
Sense, they find these things written as the beginning of all Philosophy, in obscured but ineffaceable characters, within our inmost being;
and themselves first affording any certainty and
clear meaning to that very world of Sense, by
which we endeavour to demonstrate them.

"God *is*, nay, alone *is*, for with like emphasis
we cannot say that anything else is. This is the
Absolute, the Primitively True, which the philosopher seeks. Endeavouring, by logical argu-
ment, to prove the existence of God, a Kantist
might say, would be taking out a candle to look
for the sun; nay, gaze steadily into your candle-
light, and the sun himself may be invisible. To
open the inward eye to the sight of this Primitively True; or rather we might call it, to clear
off the Obscurations of Sense, which eclipse this
truth within us, so that we may see it, and believe it not only to be true, but the foundation
and essence of all other truth,—may, in such
language as we are here using, be said to be the
problem of Critical Philosophy." *

* Carlyle's Essay on The State of German Literature, pp..67–69..

"In this point of view, Kant's system may be
thought to have a remote affinity to those of
Malebranche and Descartes. But if they in some
measure agree as to their aim, there is the widest
difference as to the means. We state what to
ourselves has long appeared the grand characteristic of Kant's Philosophy, when we mention
his distinction, seldom perhaps expressed so
broadly, but uniformly implied, between Understanding and Reason (*Verstand* and *Vernunft*).
To the Kantists, Understanding and Reason are
organs, or rather, we should say, modes of oper-
ation, by which the mind discovers Truth; but
they think that their manner of proceeding
is essentially different; that their provinces are
separable and distinguishable; nay, that it is of
the last importance to separate and distinguish
them. Reason, the Kantists say, is of a higher
nature than Understanding; it works by more
subtle methods, or higher objects, and requires
a far finer culture for its development; indeed,
in many men it is never developed at all: but
its results are no less certain, nay, rather they
are much more so; for Reason discerns Truth
itself, the absolutely and primitively *True;* while
the Understanding discerns only *relations*, and
cannot decide without *if.* The proper province
of Understanding is all, strictly speaking, *real,*

practical and material knowledge,—Mathematics,
Physics, Political Economy—the adaptation of
means to ends in the whole business of life.   In
this province it is the indispensable servant,
without which, indeed, existence itself would be
impossible.   Let it not step beyond this province,
however; not usurp the province of Reason,
which it is appointed to obey, and cannot rule
over without ruin to the whole spiritual man.
Should Understanding attempt to prove the existence of God, it ends, if thorough-going and
consistent with itself, in Atheism, or a faint possible Theism, which scarcely differs from this:
should it speculate of Virtue, it ends in *Utility*,
making Prudence and a sufficiently cunning love
of Self the highest good.   Consult Understanding
about the Beauty of Poetry, and it asks, Where
is this Beauty? or discovers it at length in
rhythms and fitnesses, and male and female
rhymes.   Witness also its everlasting paradoxes
on Necessity and the Freedom of the Will; its
ominous silence on the end and meaning of man;
and the enigma which, under such inspection,
the whole purport of existence becomes." *

Carlyle's chief interest in the efforts and results of the Kantean Philosophy in particular,

---

* Carlyle's Essay on the State of German Literature, p. 67-70.

and of German Idealism in general, concerns itself less—as a consequence of the whole tendency
of his religious views—with the "theories of perceptions" than with ethical and religious doctrines.

We do not wish to say anything of these views
which this philosophy reveals of the course and
development of the natural sciences, but we cannot refrain from stating that for those who follow it, its effects upon Ethics and Religion are
incalculable.

"The Critical Philosophy has been regarded
as the greatest intellectual achievement of the
century in which it came to light. August Wil-
helm Schlegel, whose opinion has a known value
for the English, has stated in plain terms his
belief, that in respect of its probable influence
on the moral culture of Europe, it stands on a
line with the Reformation. . . . . The noble
system of morality, the purer theology, the lofty
views of man's nature derived from it, nay, perhaps the very discussion of such matters, to which
it gave so strong an impetus, have told with remarkable and beneficial influence on the whole
spiritual character of Germany. No writer of any
importance in that country, be he acquainted or
not with the Critical Philosophy, but breathes a
spirit of devoutness and elevation more or less

directly drawn from it. Such men as Goethe and
Schiller cannot exist without effect in any literature or in any century : but if one circumstance
more than another has contributed to forward
their endeavours, and introduce that higher tone
into the literature of Germany, it has been this
philosophical system ; to which, in wisely believing its results, or even in wisely denying them,
all that was lofty and pure in the genius of poetry,
or the reason of man,. so readily allied itself. " *

Thus Carlyle attaches the very highest importance to the Kantean Philosophy. It is now
only necessary to show that, in his eyes, Kant's
great successors have no really striking differ-
ences. The only thing which in the systems of
Fichte, Schelling and Hegel, Carlyle considered
great and remarkable was the Idealism inter-
woven in them all ; in other respects he charac-
terized them simply as " these Kantean systems."

He was rather more, however, attached to
Fichte, whose manly bearing filled him with the
greatest reverence, than to any of the other
philosophers.

" The cold, colossal, adamantine spirit, standing erect and clear, like a Cato Major among
degenerate men; fit to have been the teacher of

---

* Carlyle's Essay on the State of German Literature, p. 66.

the Stoa, and to have discoursed of Beauty and
Virtue in the groves of Academe! We state
Fichte's character, as it is known and admitted
by men of all parties among the Germans, when
we say that so robust an intellect, a soul so calm,
so lofty, massive and immovable, has not mingled
in philosophical discussion since the time of
Luther. We figure his motionless look, had he
heard the charge of mysticism which was made
against him in England. For the man rises before us, amid contradiction and debate, like a
granite mountain amid clouds and wind. Ridi-
cule, of the best that could be commanded, has
been already tried against him; but it could not
avail. What was the wit of a thousand wits to
him? The cry of a thousand choughs assaulting
that old cliff of granite: seen from the summit,
these, as they winged the midway air, showed
scarce so gross as beetles, and their cry was seldom even audible. Fichte's opinions may be true
or false; but his character, as a thinker, can be
slightly valued only by such as know it ill; and
as a man, approved by action and suffering, in
his life and in his death, he ranks with a class
of men who were common only in better ages
than ours." *

----

* Carlyle's Essay on the State of German Literature, pp. 65–66. .

Carlyle's aspirations were akin to Fichte's, and as their spiritual development was similar, Fichte must have attracted Carlyle, and unconsciously exerted a great influence on him.

We should be going too far if we attempted to trace back to Fichte certain peculiarities of Carlyle's phraseology, and many of his important utterances (this was actually done in several instances by Novalis' instrumentality), but it is nevertheless worthy of remark that Carlyle's "Natural Supernaturalism" bears the strongest resemblance to Fichte's idealism.

Similar to Fichte, his doctrine—founded upon the "Divine Idea of the world which lies at the bottom of Appearances" reached its climax in the Ethical and the Religious.

And when Fichte says: "After all, this according to my doctrine, is the true character of the truly religious man. There is but one desire that swells his breast and inspires his mind—the happiness of all soul-inspired creatures. Thy kingdom come! is his prayer; besides this nothing has the least charm for him. He has become insensible to the possibility of longing for anything else. He recognizes but one way of furthering this ideal, that of following the voice of his conscience in all his actions, unwaveringly, without fear or sophistry. This links him again to the

world, not as an object of enjoyment, but as a
sphere for conscientious living pointed out by his
inner voice ; " if Fichte advances this as his ideal
of a morally religious man—an ideal, however,
which may be applied to any man—we do not
see how Carlyle's ideal could be better formulated.

The significance of Schelling's and Hegel's
systems for Carlyle retreats to the background.
Schelling's philosophy had fascinated him, to be
sure, in those days of bitter doubt, when he was
trying to formulate his own ideas of life. In his
Journal and Letters we occasionally meet with
his name, but Carlyle's opinion in regard to him
is generally expressed too vaguely for us to say
that Schelling had any permanent influence upon
his mind. He said once about him : " He is a
man evidently of deep insight into individual
things ; speaks wisely and reasons with the nicest
accuracy on all matters where we understand
his data." *

In England, Schelling's influence was much
more important on Coleridge and his followers
than on Carlyle.

In regard to Hegel Carlyle never expressed
himself even as clearly, so that his position with
reference to him cannot be any more accurately

---

* Carlyle's Essay on the State of German Literature, p. 65.

defined. "He puts a high estimation upon him," * as Froude says, and we shall soon discover that there is one subject on which the two men agree, without daring to draw any inference from it.

However greatly Carlyle respected the various representatives of German Idealism, and however deeply he was impressed by them, we must nevertheless here, at the conclusion of our reflections on his attitude toward philosophy, again call especial attention to the fact that he acknowledged no ultimate end in the whole of the idealistic systematic speculation.

In his "Essay on Characteristics," Carlyle speaks of "the disease of metaphysics," and expresses the opinion that "man is sent hither not to question, but to work;" and he even goes so far as to say that "the mere existence and necessity of a philosophy is an evil;" that except as Poetry and Religion, it would have no being.

"Metaphysical Speculation, if a necessary evil, is the forerunner of much good . . . . for of our Modern Metaphysics, accordingly, may not this already be said, that if they have produced no Affirmation, they have destroyed much Nega-

* Froude's Carlyle, vol. ii., chap. 2.

tion? It is a disease expelling a disease: the fire of Doubt, consuming away the Doubtful; that so the Certain come to light, and again lie visible on the surface. English or French Metaphysics, in reference to this last stage of the Speculative process, are not what we allude to here; but only the Metaphysics of the Germans. In France or England, since the days of Diderot and Hume, though all thought has been of a sceptico-metaphysical texture, so far as there was any Thought, we have seen no Metaphysics, but only more or less ineffectual questions whether such could be. In the Pyrrhonism of Hume and the Materialism of Diderot, Logic had, as it were, overshot itself, overset itself. Now though the athlete, to use our old figure, cannot, by much lifting, lift up his own body, he may shift it out of a laming posture, and get to stand in a free one.

"Such a service have German Metaphysics done for man's mind. The second sickness of Speculation has abolished both itself and the first. Friedrich Schlegel complains much of the fruitlessness, the tumult and transiency of German as of all Metaphysics; and with reason. Yet in that wide-spreading, deep-whirling vortex of Kantism, so soon metamorphosed into Fichteism, Schellingism, and then as Hegelism, and

Cousinism, perhaps finally evaporated, is not this issue visible enough, that Pyrrhonism and Materialism, themselves necessary phenomena in European culture, have disappeared; and a Faith in Religion has again become possible and inevitable for the scientific mind; and the word *Free*-thinker no longer means the Denier or Caviller, but the Believer, or the Ready to believe? Nay, in the higher Literature of Germany, there already lies, for him that can read it, the beginning of a new revelation of the Godlike; as yet unrecognised by the mass of the world; but waiting there for recognition, and sure to find it when the fit hour comes. This age is not wholly without its prophets." *

* Carlyle's Essay on Characteristics, pp. 35-36.

CHAPTER VII.

CARLYLE'S CONCEPTION OF POETRY AND ART IN GENERAL.

Literature is but a branch of Religion, and always participates in its character; however in our time it is the only branch that still shows any greenness; and as some think must one day become the main stem.—Carlyle's Essay on Characteristics, p. 20.

Poetry is another form of Wisdom.—Carlyle's Essay on Burns, p. 49.

"And knowest thou no Prophet, even in the vesture, environment, and dialect of this age? None to whom the Godlike had revealed itself, through all meanest and highest forms of the Common; and by him been again prophetically revealed: in whose inspired melody, even in these rag-gathering and rag-burning days, Man's Life again begins, were it but afar off, to be divine? Knowest thou none such? I know him, and name him—Goethe." *

And this it is, "in Goethe and more or less in Schiller and the rest," which gives the most

---

* Sartus Resartus, bk. iii., chap. 7.

essential feature of Carlyle's conception of the
nature of the poet. "The coldest sceptic, the
most callous worldling, sees not the actual aspects of life more sharply than they are here
delineated : the Nineteenth Century stands before us, in all its contradiction and perplexity ;
barren, mean and baleful, as we have all known
it ; yet here no longer mean and barren, but
enamelled into beauty in the poet's spirit; for
its secret significance is laid open, and thus, as
it were, the life-giving fire that slumbers in it
is called forth, and flowers and foliage, as of
old, are springing on its bleakest wilderness, and
overmantling its sternest cliffs. For these men
have not only the clear eye, but the loving heart.
They have penetrated into the mystery of Nature ;
after long trial they have been initiated ; and
to unwearied endeavour, Art has at last yielded
her secret ; and thus can the Spirit of our Age,
embodied in fair imaginations, look forth on us,
earnest and full of meaning, from their works.
As the first and indispensible condition of good
poets, they are wise and good men : much they
have seen and suffered, and they have conquered
all this, and made it all their own ; they have
known life in its heights and depths, and mas-
tered it in both, and can teach others what it
is, and how to lead it rightly. Their minds are

as a mirror to us, when the perplexed image of
our own being is reflected back in soft and clear
interpretation. Here mirth and gravity are blended together; wit rests on deep devout wisdom,
as the green-sward with its flowers must rest on
the rock, whose foundations reach downward to
the centre. In a word, they are believers; but
their faith is no sallow plant of darkness; it is
green and flowery, for it grows in the sunlight.
And this faith is the doctrine they have to teach
us, the sense which, under every noble and grace-
ful form, it is their endeavour to set forth:

> "As all Nature's thousand changes
> But one changeless God proclaim,
> So in Art's wide kingdoms ranges
> One sole meaning, still the same:
> This is Truth, eternal Reason,
> Which from Beauty takes its dress,
> And, serene through time and season,
> Stands for aye in lovliness."

Such, indeed, is the end of Poetry at all times;
yet in no recent literature known to us, except
the German, has it been so far attained; nay,
perhaps, so much as consciously and steadfastly
attempted." *

To this conception of the poet's calling which
we constantly meet with in his works, Carlyle

---

* State of German Literature, p. 56.

raised himself through the fervent study of Goethe and Schiller. One can easily picture to one's self how the Scotch peasant's son, reared among stern, primitive and very circumscribed notions of things, at first incredulously opposed Goethe's and Schiller's æsthetics. Goethe's idea of art, his "almost religious love for it" appears at first to Carlyle to be "odd, inexplicable." He imagines that in Germany, as well as in other countries, the poet is differently regarded. But in the spring of 1830 we find in his Journal—perhaps with direct bearing upon Goethe's gentle Xenie—* the following remarkable words: "Who possesses science and art, has also Religion; who does not possess either, he must have Religion."

"What *is* art and poetry? Is the beautiful higher than the good? A higher *form* thereof? Thus were a poet not only a priest, but a high-priest." "When Goethe and Schiller say or insinuate that art is higher than religion, do they mean perhaps this? That whereas religion represents (what is the essence of truth for man) the good is *infinitely* (the word is emphatic) dif-

---

* "Xenie" was a name given to satirical epigrams used by Goethe and Schiller; but the "gentle Xenie" was used solely by Goethe.

ferent from the evil, but sets them in a state
of hostility (as in heaven and hell), art likewise
admits and inculcates this quite infinite difference,
but *without* hostility, with peacefulness, like the
difference of two poles which cannot coalesce
yet do not quarrel—nay, should not quarrel, for
both are essential to the whole. In this way is
Goethe's morality to be considered as a *higher*
(apart from its comprehensiveness, nay, univer-
sality) than has hitherto been promulgated?
Sehr einseitig! And yet perhaps there is a
glimpse of the truth here." *

The germ of Goethe's and Schiller's doctrine
of the beauty and sublimity of the poet's calling,
became still further developed in Carlyle. It received nourishment through the study of Milton, to whom at this time he was devoting himself. In Milton he found—as well as the deepest
religious and puritanical sentiments—ideas which
he could bring into harmony with those of
Goethe's. He was particularly impressed by the
peculiar didactic tendency which Milton dis-
played as a poet. The nobleness of the moral
claim ennobled the question of the poet's calling
in the eyes of the primitive but prejudiced Scotch
mind; the claim that he who expressed the hope

---

* Froude's Life of Carlyle, vol. ii., p. 17.

of becoming a great poet and of writing "pure and sublime thoughts" ought himself to be "a true poem," a pattern of "the best and honourablest things." *

As Milton's ideal for the poet is not realizable in "the heat of youth or the vapours of wine," as his ideal is not supported by the "invocation of dame Memory and her siren daughters" he considers the gift lent him "but by devout prayer to that Eternal Spirit who can enrich with all utterance and knowledge, and sends out His seraphim with the hallowed fire of His altar, to touch and purify the lips of whom He pleases." †

These Miltonic ideals, which in Germany Klopstock had represented, appear to stand in sharp contrast to Goethe's and Schiller's æsthetic views, and form a very prominent part of Carlyle's.

He considers the poet to be "an inspired thinker," ‡ a soul who performs heavenly music; his mission is to sing the glory of God. True poetry is a holy, divine, inspired thing. The essential element of the poet is, according to Carlyle, religion; and this view at once makes it clear what Carlyle's standpoint is as to the question

---

* Milton's Apology for Smectymnus, (ed. Bohn) p. 118.

† Second book of Reason of Church Government, (ed. Fletcher) introductory paragraph, p. 44.

‡ Essay on the Death of Goethe.

of the relation of Poetry to Religion. Carlyle's idea here exactly coincides with Hegel's, who represents "the Fine Arts only as a degree of freedom, not as the highest freedom itself," and points out to the "Fine Arts" its "future in true religion." And when Schiller, impressed by the feeling of the highest unity of the moral, the religious and the beautiful (in the Ideal), uses the words: "The healthy and beautiful nature needs no morality, no metaphysics," * you could just as well say it needs no divine, no immortality upon which to repose and maintain itself.

This form of expression would not have met with favour in Carlyle's eyes, for he would have replied that healthy morality and religiousness needs no beauty—it has and comprehends the only true beauty in itself. It was exactly this religious element which was an inner strength to Carlyle, to the poet and to all men, giving solidity without enchaining. And if he believed that religion was the essence, the unconsciously living element of the poet, he was, nevertheless, far from wishing to make it bend to the yoke of any especial religious views. As the moral law and the moral duty do not cause man to

---

* Schiller and Goethe's Correspondence.

deteriorate, but help to elevate and give him freedom, in the same way does the Divine, if it penetrates the poet, not oppress, but gives him its sanction.

"Ever must the Fine Arts be if not religion, yet indissolubly united to it, dependent on it, virtually blended with it, as body is with soul." *

"Poetry is but another form of Wisdom, of Religion; is itself Wisdom and Religion," that "unspeakable beauty which in its highest clearness is Religion." †

These utterances, and those which follow, show that Carlyle's views are not materially different from Goethe's: "Art rests upon a sort of religious sense, upon a deep, immutable earnestness, on account of which it so willingly is united to Religion. Religion needs no Art-Sense—it rests upon its own earnestness," but it gives as little as it produces. ‡ And his aphorisms on the History of the Arts, of the year 1808, we by no means wish to quote as a mere expression of a view: "Art has, properly speaking, originated out of and in Religion." §

---

* Carlyle's Essay on Jesuitism, p. 271.
† Carlyle's Essay on History.
‡ Sprüche in Prosa, (Leoper) p. 690.
§ Op. cit., p. 147.

That Carlyle did not at all make the poetical endowment dependent on the religious feeling, must be explicitly stated, for it is not by any means a gift to clothe the religious feeling in verse.

"Poetry is Inspiration: has in it a certain spirituality—it is no separate faculty, no organ which can be superadded to the rest, or disjoined from them; but rather the result of their general harmony and completeness. The feelings, the gifts that exist in the Poet are those that exist in every human soul. The imagination which shudders at the Hell of Dante, is the same faculty, weaker in degree, which called that picture into being. How does the Poet speak to men, with power, but by being still more a man than they?" *

Carlyle seems to prefer to designate the poet by one word—Vates—which he again and again uses. Let us try to comprehend his ideal.

"The true poet is ever, as of old, the Seer; whose eye has been gifted to discern the godlike mystery of God's Universe, and to decipher some new lines of its celestial writing; we can still call him a Vates and Seer; for he *sees* into this greatest of secrets, 'the open secret;' hidden

---

* Essay on Burns, vol. ii., p. 18.

things become clear; how the future (both resting on Eternity) is but another phase of the Present: thereby are his words in very truth prophetic; what he has spoken shall be done." *

The greatest gift which can fall to the lot of one man—as Prophet and Seer—fell to the "Vates:" that of revealing "Poetic Beauty." † "As the material Seer is the eye and revealer of all things, so is Poetry, so is the World-Poet, in a spiritual sense." ‡ He, the World-Poet, is the only true interpreter of the invisible, the Eternal, as it is revealed in the world. He has not far to seek for material, for the ideal world is not separated from the material world, but permeates and fills it.

"Wherever there is a sky above him, and a world around him, the poet is in his place; for here, too, is man's existence, with its infinite longings and small requirings; its ever-thwarted, ever-renewed endeavours, its unspeakable aspirations, its fears and hopes that wander through Eternity; and all the mystery of brightness and of gloom that it was ever made of, in any age or climate, since man first began to live. Is there

---

* Essay on Death of Goethe, p. 44.
† Biography, p. 59.
‡ Essay on Death of Goethe, p. 43.

not the fifth act of a Tragedy in every death-
bed, though it were a peasant's, and a bed of
heath? And are wooings and weddings obsolete,
that there can be Comedy no longer? Or are
men suddenly grown wise, that Laughter must no
longer shake his sides, but be cheated of his
Farce? Man's life and nature is, as it was, and
as it ever will be. But the poet must have an
eye to read these things, and a heart to understand them; or they come and pass away before him in vain. He is a *Vates*, a seer; a gift
of vision has been given him. Has life no meanings for him, which another cannot equally decipher; then he is no poet, and Delphi itself
will not make him one." *

Prophet and Poet are for Carlyle of one stock,
and according to his opinion it is only an indi-
cation of a perversely developed epoch which
could be blinded to this unity.

"They both have penetrated into the sacred
mystery of the Universe; what Goethe calls
'the open secret.' 'The *open* secret,' open to
all, seen by almost none! That divine mystery,
which lies everywhere in all Beings, the 'Divine
Idea of the World,' that which lies at the 'bottom of appearance,' as Fichte styles it; of which

---

* Essay on Burns, p. 13.

all appearances, from the starry sky to the grass
of the field, but especially the Appearance of
Man and his work, is but the *vesture*, the em-
bodiment that renders it visible. This mystery
is in all times and in all places; veritably is.
In most times and places it is greatly overlooked;
and the Universe, definable always in one or the
other dialect, as the realised Thought of God,
is considered as a trivial, inert, commonplace
matter,—as if, says the Satirist, it were a dead
thing, which some upholsterer had put together!
It could do no good, at present, to *speak* much
about this; but it is a pity for every one of us
if we do not know it, live ever in the knowledge
of it. Really a most mournful pity;—a failure
to live at all, if we live otherwise! But now, I
say, whoever may forget this divine mystery,
the *Vates*, whether Prophet or Poet, has penetrated into it; is a man sent hither to make it
more impressively known to us. That always
is his message; he is to reveal that to us,—
that sacred mystery which he, more than others,
lives ever present with. While others forget it,
he knows it; I might say, he has been driven
to know it; without consent asked of *him*, he
finds himself living in it, bound to live in it.
Once more, here is no Hearsay, but a direct
Insight and Belief; this man, too, could not help

being a sincere man! Whoever may live in the
shows of things, it is for him a necessity of nature
to live in the very fact of things. A man once
more, in earnest with the Universe, though all
others were but toying with it. He is a *Vates*,
first of all, in virtue of being sincere. So far
Poet and Prophet, participators in the 'open secret,' are one.

"With respect to their distinction again: The
Vates Prophet, we might say, has siezed that
sacred mystery rather on the moral side, as Good
and Evil, Duty and Prohibition; the *Vates* Poet
on what the Germans call the æsthetic side, as
Beautiful, and the like. The one we call a revealer of what we are to do; the other of what
we are to love. But indeed these two provinces
run into one another, and cannot be disjoined.
The Prophet, too, has his eye on what we are
to love: how else shall he know what it is we are
to do? The highest Voice ever heard on this
earth said withal: 'Consider the lilies of the
field; they toil not, neither do they spin: yet
Solomon in all his glory was not arrayed like
one of these'—a glance, that, into the deepest
deep of Beauty. 'The lilies of the field,'—dressed
finer than earthly princes, springing up there
in the humble furrow-field; a beautiful *eye* look-
ing-out on you, from the great inner Sea of

Beauty! How could the rude Earth make these, if her Essence, rugged as she looks and is, were not inwardly Beauty? In this point of view, too, a saying of Goethe's, which has staggered several, may have meaning: 'This Beautiful,' he intimates, 'is higher than the Good; the Beautiful includes in it the Good.' The *true* Beautiful; which, however, I have said somewhere, 'differs from the *false* as Heaven does from Vauxhall!'" *

This research of Carlyle's apparently only leads to the conclusion that there is no difference between *true* poetry and "*true* speech, not poetical," but Carlyle does not disappoint us here.

"On this point many things have been written, especially by the late German Critics, some of which are not very intelligible at first. They say, for example, that the Poet has an *infinitude* in him; communicates an *Unendlichkeit*, a certain character of 'infinitude,' to whatsoever he delineates. This, though not very precise, yet in so vague a matter is worth remembering: if well meditated, some meaning will gradually be found in it. For my own part, I find considerable meaning in the old vulgar distinction of Poetry being *metrical*, having music in it, being a Song.

---

* Carlyle's Lecture on Heroes, pp. 75-76.

Truly, if pressed to give a definition, one might say this as soon as anything else: If your delineation be authentically *musical*, musical not in the word only, but in heart and substance, in all the thoughts and utterances of it, in the whole conception of it, then it will be poetical; if not, not.—Musical: how much lies in that! A *musical* thought is one spoken by a mind that has penetrated into the inmost heart of the thing; detected the inmost mystery of it, namely, the *melody* that lies hidden in it; the inward harmony of coherence which is its soul, whereby it exists, and has a right to be, here in this world. All inmost things, we may say, are melodious; naturally utter themselves in Song. The meaning of Song goes deep. Who is there that, in logical words, can express the effect that music has on us? A kind of inarticulate unfathomable speech, which leads us to the edge of the Infinite, and lets us for moments gaze into that! All speech, even the commonest speech, has something of song in it: not a parish in the world but has its parish-accent;—the rhythm or *tune* to which the people there *sing* what they have to say! Accent is a kind of chanting; all men have an accent of their own,—though they only *notice* that of others. . , . . All deep things are Song. It seems somehow the very central essence of us, Song; as if the rest were but wrappage and hulls! The primal element of us; of us and of all things. The Greeks fabled of Sphere-Harmonies: it was the feeling they had of the inner structure of Nature; that the soul of all her voices and utterances was perfect music. Poetry, therefore, we will call *musical Thought*. The Poet is he who *thinks* in that manner. At bottom, it turns still on the power of intellect; it is a man's sincerity and depth of vision that makes him a Poet. See deep enough, and you see musically; the heart of Nature *being* everywhere music, if you can only reach it." *

So the poet is, according to Carlyle, naturally the deepest of all thinkers. Poetry is insight, a higher knowledge; the true thinker alone is the poet, the Seer. Heavenly wisdom possesses his Soul, fills his heart: it is the North Star which guides him through life independent of external success or of external worldly results.

"We often hear of this and the other external condition being requisite for the existence of a poet. Sometimes it is a certain sort of training;

* On Heroes, p. 78.

he must have studied certain things, studied, for instance, 'the elder dramatists,' and so learned a poetic language; as if poetry lay in the tongue, not in the heart. At other times we are told he must be bred in a certain rank, and must be on a confidential footing with the higher classes; because, above all things, he must see the world. As to seeing the world, we apprehend this will cause him little difficulty, if he have but eyesight to see it with. . . . . The mysterious workmanship of man's heart, the true light and the inscrutable darkness of man's destiny, reveal themselves not only in capital cities and crowded saloons, but in every hut and hamlet where men have their abode." *

It was "not personal enjoyment," freedom from care and a merry, jovial life which made him great, "but a high, heroic idea of Religion, of Patriotism, of heavenly Wisdom, in one or the other form, in which cause he neither shrank from suffering, nor called on the earth to witness it as something wonderful; but patiently endured, counting it blessedness enough so to spend and be spent." †

On this subject Carlyle is continually waging

---

* Essay on Burns, pp. 13–14.
† Op. cit., p. 48.

an internecine war against those whom he calls
the "sweet singers." The poet's task is not to
offer "pleasant singing" and to prepare "de-
lights" for the indolent. When "Fine Literature" concerns itself with "the unspeakable
glories and rewards of pleasing its generation,"
it becomes a degradation to Art, and has as little
to do with it as where united with every pomp
of the opera, of the stage and of music, it solely
tries to become a slave to the vile amusement of
the epoch.

This explains Carlyle's merciless and often too
severe judgment of almost all his contemporaries
in English Literature. With the exception of
Tennyson, Ruskin, Browning, Arthur Clough and
a few others, his judgment is almost entirely an
unfavourable one. The measure which he used
in forming an estimate of his ideal poets, Homer,
Æschulus, Dante, Shakspeare, Milton, Goethe
and Schiller, he applied to all other poets in
order to determine their absolute significance in
history. Even such men as Byron and Burns,
the latter especially his favourite, did not escape
this tribunal.

His judgment of the professional, literary and
art critics supplies us with further information
as to his conception of the relation of poetry and
art in general. To quibble about a poem or an

art work was not only distasteful to him, but appeared a manifest hypocrisy and lie.

"The Fine Arts become a Throne of Hypocrisy." Falsehood reigns here sovereign, and covers the abyss with sparkling words. "The Fine Arts, wherever they turn up as *business*, whatever Committee sit upon them, are sure to be parent of much empty talk, labourious hypocrisy, dillettanteism, futility; involving huge trouble and expense, and babble, which end in no result, if not in worse than none." *

This single quotation is quite sufficient here. What justifies him in this anger is his own worth. His savage mood knows no boundaries in the attack against this modern "art-lie." The kernel of truth in this warfare is easily recognized and will retain its value, for certainly it will forever be better "to perambulate through a picture-gallery with little or no speech; † but on the other hand, however, it must be strongly emphasized that Carlyle's understanding of Art and interest in Art—so far as the plastic arts are concerned—was neither sufficiently versatile nor great to give an independent and worthy judgment.

---

* Jesuitism, p. 272.
† Carlyle's Life of Sterling, chap. 7.

Schiller was not ashamed to confess (in a letter
to Humboldt, written on February 17th, 1803)
that "Italy and Rome are no countries for me;
the mere 'matter' [das Physische] would oppress
me, and the *æsthetic* would give me no delight,
because an interest and feeling for the. plastic
arts is wanting in me"—and similar was it with
Carlyle, although he did not so openly acknowl-
edge it, and would not modify his severe judgment of the "Gallery and Cathedral Visitors"* in
Rome, when his criticism really only touches the
fashionable foolery, and cannot at all be applied
to such a spirit as Sterling, whose deepest in-
terests in life were linked to the plastic arts. *

The only work of art for which Carlyle really
had a most perfect understanding and interest
was the portrait, his deep interest in which is
proved already by the fact that it was he who
first proposed the establishment of a national
portrait gallery in Scotland. (He had sorely
missed such an one in Berlin, where he had
tried to become familiar with the time of Frederick the Great.) Further was this shown in a
high degree in an Essay on the various portraits
of John Knox. We seem too unappreciative of
these delicate observations which we are indebted

* Carlyle's Life of Sterling, pp. 148–154.

to his pen for. It is sufficient here, however, to merely draw attention to his words on Cranach's portraits of Luther. The walls of his study were completely covered by the best and the most interesting portraits which he could procure of all his "heroes."

CHAPTER VIII.

CARLYLE'S ATTITUDE TOWARD HISTORY.

A confession made by Carlyle in his Journal of 1842—of the publication of which he never dreamed—admits us into the most secret recesses of his thought and feeling: "Of Dramatic Art, though I have eagerly listened to a Goethe speaking of it, and to several hundreds of others mumbling and trying to speak of it, I find that I, practically speaking, know yet almost as good as nothing. Indeed, of Art generally, (*Kunst*, so called) I *can* almost know nothing. My first and last secret of *Kunst* is to get a thorough *intelligence* of the *fact* to be painted, represented, or, in whatever way, set forth—the *fact* deep as Hades, high as heaven, and written *so*, as to the visual face of it upon our poor earth. This once blazing within me, if it will ever get to blaze, and bursting to be out, one has to take the whole dexterity of adaptation one is master of, and with tremendous struggling, contrive to exhibit it, one way or the other. This is not *Art*, I know well." *

All of Carlyle's natural endowments led him into other channels than those of art in its ordinary sense: in history, in the study of mankind, he found the arrangement of the Eternal most beautifully and divinely revealed. God was to him the only Artist whose works he cared to study with a religious and respectful spirit. Nature was great and divine, but man seemed to him the divinest creation, and of man's life, his growth and development, his struggles and aspirations, his faithful toil, his good fortune, his misfortune, and his final passing away, as it repeats itself over and over again in the course of history, in powerful changes and yet in perpetual unity, that was to him "the eternal, constant Gospel" which his soul thirsted to understand, which filled his heart with poetry, which stimulated every nerve, and which broke forth in all his works, and—although written in prose—made genuine poetic creations.

History and the writing of history—considered from Carlyle's point of view—was the proper field of activity for Carlyle's mind. He not only devoted the greater portion of his life and his best

---

* Froude's Life of Carlyle, Franklin Square Ed., vol. iii., p. 40.

years to it, but was indebted to it for his repu-
tation.

The following quotations show his comprehension of history: "In the one little Letter of
Æneas Sylvius there is more of history than in
all of Robertson." * "The thing I want to see
is not Red Book Lists and Court Calendars, and
Parliamentary Registers, but the Life of Man:
what men did and thought, suffered, enjoyed;
the form, especially the spirit, of their terrestrial
existence, its outward environment, its inward
principle; *how* and *what* it was; whence it pro-
ceeded, whither it was tending.   Mournful, in
truth, is it to behold what the business called
'History,' in these so enlightened and illuminated times, still continues to be.   Can you gather
from it, read till your eyes go out, any dimmest
shadow of an answer to that great question:
How men lived and had their being; were it but
economically, as, what wages they got, and what
they bought with these?" †

History does not consist in relating court in-
trigues and stories of Prime Ministers and their
countries; it does not consist in the conscientious
binding together of deeds or the best representa-

---

* Carlyle's Essay on Boswell's Life of Johnson, p. 84.
† Loc. cit.

tion of the development of the forms of State;
the object of the historian is to represent the
inner conditions of life, the conscious and unconscious aspirations of mankind, which are never
alike in two dissimilar ages. Not alone battles
and war tumults, not alone laws and constitutions
and their developments, which, nevertheless, "are
not our Life, but only the house wherein our Life
is led." *   To contemplate all the long-forgotten
and concealed acts and phenomena of the human
species, to penetrate 'reverently' the spiritual
and physical nature, to depict what is of promise,
that is task set before the historian.

The most important part of history is, perhaps,
not for one person to relate it in general, "for as
all Action is, by its nature, to be figured as ex-
tended in breadth and depth, as well as in length;
that is to say, is based on Passion and Mystery, if
we investigate its origin; and spreads abroad on
all hands, modifying and modified; as well as
advances towards completion,—so all narrative
is, by nature, of only one dimension; only travels
forward towards us, or towards successive points:
Narrative is *linear*, Action is *solid*.   Also for our
'chains,' or chainlets, of 'canvas and effects,'"
which we so assiduously track through certain

_____
* Carlyle's Essay on History, p. 255.

hand-breadths of years and square miles, when
the whole is a broad, deep Immensity, and each
atom is 'chained' and complected with all!
Truly, if History is Philosophy teaching by experience, the writer fitted to compose History is
hitherto an unknown man. The Experience itself would require All-knowledge to record it,—
were the All-wisdom needful for such Philosophy as would interpret it to be had for ask-
ing. Better were it that mere earthly Histori-
ans should lower such pretensions, more suitable
for Reminiscence than for human science; and
aiming only at some picture of the things acted,
which picture itself will at best be a poor approx-
imation, leave the inscrutable purport of them
an acknowledged secret; or at most, in reverent
Faith, far different from that teaching of Philosophy, pause over the mysterious vestige of
Him, whose path is in the great deep of Time,
whom History indeed reveals, but only all History, and in Eternity, will clearly reveal." *

These opinions do not blunt the ardour of the
investigator; they only inspire him with a desire
to search more and more into the past. "Let all
men explore it as the true fountain of knowledge;
by whose light alone, consciously or unconscious-

---

* Carlyle's Essay on History, p. 258.

ly employed, can the Present or the Future be interpreted or guessed." *

This ideal of the science of history admits of a distinction between the Artist and Artisan; the one 'labours' mechanically in his department without turning his eye upon the whole, perhaps without feeling that there is a whole; the other informs and ennobles the humblest sphere in life with an idea of the whole, and habitually knows that only in the whole is the partial to be truly discerned. The tasks and the duties of these two are entirely different, and each has his definite work, "The simple husbandman can till his field, and by knowledge he has gained of its soil, sow it with the fit grain, though the deep rocks and central fires are unknown to him: his little crop hangs under and over the firmament of stars, and sails through untracked celestial spaces, between Aries and Libra; nevertheless it ripens for him in due season and he gathers it safe into his barn. As a husbandman he is blameless in disregarding those higher wonders; but as a thinker, and faithful inquirer into Nature, he were wrong. So, likewise, is it with the Historian, who examines some special aspect of History; and from this or that combination of

---

* Carlyle's Essay on History, p. 258.

circumstances,—political, moral, economical,—and the issues it has led to, infers that such and such properties belong to human society; and that the like circumstances will produce the like issue; which inference, if other trials confirm it, must be held true and practically valuable.   He is wrong only, and an artisan, when he fancies that these properties, discovered or discoverable, exhaust the matter; and sees not at every step, that it is inexhaustible.

"However, that class of cause-and-effect speculators, with whom no wonder would remain wonderful, but all things in Heaven and Earth must be computed and 'accounted for;' and even the Unknown, the Infinite in man's Life, had under the words *enthusiasm, superstition, spirit of the age*, and so forth, obtained, as it were, an algebraical symbol and given value,— have now well-nigh played their part in European culture; and may be considered, as in most countries, even in England itself, where they linger the latest, verging toward extinction." *

"The Political Historian, once almost the sole cultivator of History, has now found various associates, who strive to elucidate other phases of human Life; of which, as hinted above, the

---

* Carlyle's Essay on History, p. 259.

political conditions it is passed under are but one, and though the primary, perhaps not the most important, of the many outward arrangements. Of this Historian himself, moreover, in his own special department, new and higher things are beginning to be expected. From of old, it was too often to be reproachfully observed of him, that he dwelt with disproportionate fondness in Senate-houses, in Battle-fields, nay, even in Kings' Antechambers; forgetting that far away from such scenes, the mighty tide of Thought and Action was still rolling on its wondrous course, in gloom and brightness; and in its thousand remote valleys, a whole world of Existence, with or without an earthly sun of Happiness to warm it, with or without a heavenly sun of Holiness to purify and sanctify it, was blossoming and fading, whether the 'famous victory' were won or lost. The time seems coming when much of this must be amended." *

What ennobled history for Carlyle was the "Infinite in human Life," the highest revelation of the divine Spirit, as it was revealed and was to be seen in human nature. "Wherever there is a Man, a God also is revealed, and all that is Godlike: a whole epitome of the Infinite with

---

* Carlyle's Essay on History, pp. 259-260.

its meanings, lies enfolded in the Life of every man." *

To discern truly this revelation, a "seer" was, of course, necessary: and it is just here where, according to Carlyle, the same talent must become a part of both the poet and the truly great historian.   This is the point at which history becomes true poetry, where true poetry consists in the right interpretation of truth, and of fact. †

Poetry, in the sense of fiction, of idle "invention," is not comparable with truth; the poet's invention does not consist in the creation of dreamy and fanciful forms; it consists rather in the after-creation, in the new revelation of divine thought, as it lies at the foundation of the appearances of the world and the world's history. "An Æschylus or a Sophocles sang the *truest* (which was also the divinest) they had been privileged to discover here below." ‡

According to Carlyle's idea, only a Shakspeare or a Homer can discover the infinite meaning of history, of human life. The true historical writing is that "mighty, world-old Rhapsodia of Existence, the grand, sacred Epos, or Bible of World-History, infinite in meaning as the Divine

---

* Essay on Biography, p. 58.
† Essay on Boswell's Life of Johnson, p. 82.
‡ Essay on The Opera, p. 124.

Mind it Emblems; wherein he is wise that can read here a line, and there a line." *

"Great men are the inspired Texts of that divine Book of Revelation." † They, the great men, the "heroes," to use Carlyle's terminology, give their intrinsic worth to the world and the world's history; they are the heart, the kernel around which everything revolves; they are, in a certain sense, the creators of everything which the mass of people perform; they give the ideals, and are the soul of the world's history. ‡

We pause here where the celebrated and variously maligned *Hero - Worship* offers an explanation.

Carlyle's Hero-Worship rests upon the conviction that (if the germ of the Divine is innate in mankind yet) only the chosen, the "Heroes," whose duty it is to bring truth to victory, are sent from heaven to awaken dormant powers, the heroes whose command the world must listen to, for their message comes directly from heaven. It is this belief of Carlyle's, finding representatives among the leading minds of every age, which, followed out even in great ruggedness, cannot possibly be settled by the once thrown

---

* Essay on Count Cagliostro, p. 65.

† Sartor Resartus, bk. ii., p. 122.

‡ Essay on Heroes, i.

out vindication of mere strength and force. It is not here the place to examine more critically this charge; even as little is it the place to explain the difference of Carlyle's principles from those of Buckle. It is sufficient to point out that Carlyle never was a representative of mere "strength and force." He recognizes only one power, and that is truth and morality; a truth whose victory must be won by every sacrifice, by life and by blood; whose victory is the certain hope of all human struggles and battles. "*Right* is the eternal symbol of *might*." Right gives might and power—is his motto, indeed. *Right* shall carry off the victory which *might* has won. With this belief in the victory of good over evil in the long run; in the victory of good as the hero aspires to it, and for which the hero sacrifices himself, stands or falls his whole view of life. We see that this cheerful and noble recognition of "the heroic" in history can frighten only the indolent nature into moral lethargy.

Considered from Carlyle's standpoint, the lesson which history teaches is unparalleled: the world's history is a message from the past to teach us to understand the present and the future; it consists—as Kingsley has expressed it—*

---

* And Kingsley's words are, indeed, the formulation of Carlyle's ideas.

132   THOMAS CARLYLE.

" in the overwhelming and yet ennobling knowledge that there was such a thing as Duty, first
taught me to see in history, not the mere farce-
tragedy of man's crimes and follies, but the deal-
ings of a righteous Ruler of the Universe, whose
ways are in the great deep, and whom the sin
and errors, as well as the virtues and discoveries
of man, must obey and justify."

In this way Aristotle's comparison of the poet
and historian finds explanation with Carlyle.
If the task is pointed out, then to the historian,* τὰ γενόμενα λέγειν, and to the poet to represent οἷα ἂν γένοιτο, and if δὶο καὶ φιλοσοφώτερον καὶ
σπευδαιότερον ποίησις ἱστορίας ἐστίν, Carlyle, with
his immutable views of the invariable government, according to the moral principles of an
always judicial God, would have nothing to say
but that, in general, only the "philosophical and
the earnest man" is able to understand the
world's history, that the task to consider what
"might have happened" or "ought to have
happened" was far beyond the capacity of any
man, but that it belonged to every man to seri-
ously endeavour to understand the revelation of
God and the Universe *as it exists*, and history
as it takes place before our very eyes; to under-

* Poetics, ix.

stand that there is no "greater truth" and no
smaller truth, but only *one* truth, and that the
one revealed in the world's history, in the history
of mankind; truths, to be sure, only discernable
to the wise, to the true poet and the true historian, whose common ideal is the recognition of
exactly this thing, which each in his own way
strives to reach and to teach to a struggling
world.   Thus does Carlyle apprehend the higher,
indeed, the highest unity of poet and historian,
a unity which consists in this common ideal, although their ways of expressing it may be different, a unity that would elude every eye—but
which was seen and felt and expressed by Goethe
himself :

> " Wer in der Weltgeschichte lebt,
>   Dem Augenblick soll't er sich richten ?
>   Wer in die Zeiten schaut und strebt,
>   Nur der ist wert, zu sprechen und zu dichten."

CHAPTER IX.

CARLYLE'S ETHICS.

"The Gospel of Work."

Man must work as well as worship.—Sartor Resartus, p. 250.

With those . . . . who in true manful endeavour, were it under despotism or under sansculottism, create somewhat, with those alone, in the end, does the hope of the world lie.—Carlyle's Essay on Goethe's Works, p. 182.

After having attempted to comprehend the various and important aspects of Carlyle's views, there only remains for us now the task of grasping, in as few words as possible, his complete moral doctrines which have been expressed by himself in the simplest and best manner:

"Love not Pleasure, love God! This is the Everlasting Yea, wherein all contradiction is solved; wherein whoso walks and works, it is well with him." *

The *duty* laid upon us by God to recognize the moral "work" enjoined upon us by heaven,

---

* Sartor Resartus, p. 133.

and to perform this according to our light, that
is the familiar doctrine which Carlyle, with his
whole energy, with each page which he wrote,
tried to preach afresh to the world.

The first step to the fulfilment of this duty is
the recognition of it.

"If called to define Shakspeare's faculty, I
should say superiority of Intellect, and think I
had included all under that. . . . . We talk
of faculties as if they were distinct things separable; as if a man had intellect, imagination, fancy,
etc., as he has hands, feet, and arms. That is a
capital error. Then, again, we hear of a man's
'intellectual nature,' and of his 'moral nature,'
as if these, again, were divisible, and existed apart.
. . . . We ought to know withal, and to keep
forever in mind that these divisions are at bottom
but *names;* that man's spiritual nature, the vital
Force which dwells in him, is essentially one and
indivisible ; that what we call imagination, fancy,
understanding, and so forth, are but different fig-
ures of the same Power of Insight, all indissolubly connected with each other, physiognomically
related. . . . . Morality itself, what we call
the moral quality of a man, what is this but
another *side* of the one vital Force whereby he
is and works? All that a man does is physi-
ognomical of him. You may see how a man

would fight by the way in which he sings; his
courage, or want of courage, is visible in the
word he utters, in the opinion he has formed,
no less than in the stroke he strikes. He is *one;*
and preaches the same Self abroad in all these
ways. Without hands a man might have feet,
and could still walk; but, consider it,—without
morality, intellect were impossible for him; a
thoroughly immoral *man* could not know anything at all. To know a thing, what we can call
knowing, a man must first *love* the thing, sym-
pathise with it: that is, be *virtuously* related to
it. If he have not the justice to put down his
own selfishness at every turn, the courage to stand
by the dangerous—true at every turn, how shall
he know? His virtues, all of them, will lie recorded in his knowledge. Nature, with her truth,
remains to the bad, to the selfish and the pusil-
lanimous forever a sealed book: what such can
know of Nature is mean, superficial, small: for
the uses of the day merely." *

This absolute unity of the moral and the spiritual man gives significance to the correct view of
life; true recognition of moral duty (which, if
unconscious, exists in the soul most beautifully)
leads to morality, so that spiritual greatness is

* Lectures on Heroes, pp. 98–99.

exceptionally a moral one, and the spiritual rank of a nation brings with it moral greatness as a certain result.

The first moral act which is obligatory to man, is " Renunciation," " Annihilation of Self," * the giving up of all ideas and hopes which moie or less have in view happiness for one's own self. One's first duty is to subordinate one's own pleasure, one's own well-being to the great everlasting end which heaven has set before us.

This command appears severe and grim, but is at the same time " beautiful and awful ; " * it demands infinite labour, infinite pains ; " a life of ease is not for any man or any God ; " this struggle, this " work " brings blessedness and perfects mankind ; it is the true commandment, the essence of all religion ; it can only be instilled into us when the consciousness of the eternal fills our lives. " For the son of man there is no noble crown, but is a crown of thorns ! " †

" Life is earnest," was one of Carlyle's favourite mottoes ; but if the path of duty is rough and stony, and the battles bitter, it is nevertheless destiny divinely imposed upon us, and although annihilation of self, and renunciation binds us

---

* Sartor Resartus, p. 132.

† Essay on Sir Walter Scott, p. 39.

‡ Past and Present, p. 132.

and our age conditionally, Carlyle declares with reference to what Goethe and Schiller had taught him that a "higher morality" still rests in the lap of time, a morality which leads all that is painful, troublesome and harsh in humanity to perfectness, and into harmony with the divine and the "eternally beautiful." *

In the distant future Carlyle hopes that this harmony of the divine and the human will exist upon earth, will be the condition of all men whose first and individual duty now is, without murmuring, to strive after the fulfilment of the divine duty of morality. †

This unconditional belief that harsh and stern duty is "sent by God" gives "a world of strength in return for a world of hard struggle." ‡

This is the teaching of Carlyle's life and works.

---

* Carlyle's Essay on Biography, p. 56.

† Carlyle's words remind us of the beautiful prophecy with which Emerson closes his "Address," delivered before the Senior Class in Divinity College, Cambridge, July 15, 1838 : "I look for the new Teacher, that shall follow so far those shining laws, that he shall see them come full circle; shall see their rounding complete grace ; shall see the world to be the mirror of the soul ; shall see the identity of the law of gravitation with purity of heart ; and shall show that the Ought, that Duty, is one thing with Science, with Beauty and with Joy." Here is to be found the secret to Emerson's and Carlyle's friendship.

‡ Carlyle's Essay on Characteristics, p. 25.

Froude says in his Life of Carlyle: "Carlyle believed that every man had a special duty to do in this world. If he had been asked what especially he conceived his own duty to be, he would have said that it was to force men to realize once more that the world was actually governed by a just God; that the old familiar story, acknowledged everywhere in words on Sundays, and disregarded or denied openly on week-days, was, after all, true. His writings, every one of them, his essays, his lectures, his "History of the French Revolution," his "Cromwell," even his "Frederick," were to the same purpose and on the same text—that truth must be spoken and justice must be done; on any other conditions no real commonwealth, no common welfare, is permitted or possible." *

We shall conclude these remarks on Carlyle with the same words which he uttered upon the occasion of Goethe's death: "Precious is the new light of Knowledge which our Teacher conquers for us; yet small to the new light of Love which also we derive from him: the most important element of any man's performance is the Life he has accomplished. Under the intellect-

---

* Froude's Life of Carlyle, Franklin Square Edition, vol. iii., p. 49.

zal union of man and man, which works by pre-
cept, lies a holier union of affection, working by
example; the influence of which latter, mystic,
deep-reaching, all-embracing, can still less be
computed. For Love is ever the beginning of
Knowledge, as fire is of light; and works also
more in the manner of *fire*. That Goethe was a
great Teacher of men means already that he was
a good man." *

According to our innermost conviction, we can
and must apply this to Carlyle. His infirmities
and deficiencies—which he himself in the last
years of his life was inclined to assail too severely, but which was natural to a man whose moral
claims were of such greatness, and to a man of
his excitability of disposition—his faults and his
exaggerations, his enigmatic melancholy, which so
often embittered the pleasures of life for himself
and those about him; all this, which has been
so forcibly and willingly portrayed by his adversaries, and is so easy to portray; all this, is not
able to cloud a picture of this magnificent man
which lives in the hearts of his admirers. "When
he is fully known, he will not be loved or admired
the less because he had infirmities like the rest
of us." †

---

* Carlyle's Essay on the Death of Goethe, p. 48.
† Froude's Life of Carlyle, vol. i, Introduction.